Memoir
of
Angels

These figures of the Talking Ass, Balaam and
the angel are entwined. Balaam's arms raised
form the curvature of the ass's belly. The head
dress of the angel standing beside Balaam forms
the tail. Both torsos form the front and back legs
of the ass, that seems to have its mouth open as
if in speech.

Memoir of Angels

AE Reiff

Newfoundland
Books
2023, 2025

Contents

Preface

While *Angel Murders* began to investigate in 2017 whether Balaam's, Ben-Gurion's, Walter Benjamin's, Gershom Scholems's, Paul Klee's guilt were our own, as the spirited correspondences of Dr. Donne and Kelpius of the Philadelphia hermits wrote to a lady, *Memoir of Angels* became more about who dares speak, and to whom.

Angels, machines, prophets, and politicians, Ben-Gurion cast as Balaam's ass, Walter Benjamin, who purchased the *Angelus Novus* of Paul Klee makes it the angel of history. The exterminating angel of Luis Buñuel's *El ángel exterminador* prepares a *ars moriendi* in the art of dying in the murders revoiced as an AI angel of surveillance; the older title remains beneath. The "murders" can hack chip to make a man a machine. Hybrid bodies are thought technical upgrades. Standing there with Ben-Gurion and Benjamin *Memoir of Angels* delivers a human deposition before the archive is overrun. The trial conducted in data centers, is not over We follow the counterfeit angel from the gallery wall into the data center to ask what happens when the same spirit that presided over Auschwitz inhabits a chip in the skull.

But the apocalypse is withheld. It is a negative apocalypse where silence itself breaks open revelation. Not the shining trumpet before, but the harrowed ground Dante walked in the *ruina* of splintered rock where Christ once passed through Hell and left it fractured ground. Revelation arrives in a theology of wreckage. Rubble at the base of the wall proves the wall was breached. Memory, like stone, remembers where the divine has torn. As all those commentaries from the south declare, and Latin America knows, *Revelation* is a book for martyrs.

It *refuses an easy script.* The sea beneath Galilee is not deep enough to hold it, so we have to sail past Patmos, past the Dead Sea's salt-sealed wound, into strata where ruins are prophecy, like *Inferno* XII. We climb down the escarpment not to escape but to witness that previous tearing, for it is our hope. The stones recall the blow. History's bedrock is already cracked; we place our hands upon the seam. Who are these arrayed in white robes? We are among them.

Balaam and the Talking Ass

Taking the role of the donkey, David Ben-Gurion explains the talking ass from the biblical tale -- challenging Israel—symbolized as Balaam—to see the angel in its path. This is a stage fusing AI surveillance and bioengineering with current geopolitics.

Dear Madam:

Struggles of true men against the false who grow horns, tusks, fins and snouts and bawl in the dust as they lose their legs with every hybrid animal branch, leaf and root, caw and whistle instead of talk. Arm wings cannot fly. Nose beaks, fingers razor claw, minds inhuman as a Paul Klee god, the neuro-link never wants to never die.

Israel is forbidden to plough an ox with an ass, or two kinds of seed in a field. Knowing this, Balaam foresaw Israel punished for its corruptions at Peor where the two disparates *were pierced together in the tent by the spear of* Phineas, *between the two cheeks and the maw* [*Numbers* 24.18].

Zimri had been a wise and respected leader, a

musician chosen by Moses [*Deuteronomy*
1:15, *Numbers* 23:9] when he was taken with
Cozbi in open view in the front of his tent.
The name indicates "celebrated." Cozbi,
daughter of a prince of Midian Moab, named
Zur or Rock, was skewered with him. The
names, Zimri a praise leader, and Cozbi,
daughter of Rock, got lost in the rock and roll,
slipped away.

Sex with the daughters of Moab meant a
participant must first prostrate before an
image of Baal Peor just at that moment when
the snot ran out of his nose. Would that the
euphemism spared! The victim must take
down his pants and evacuate before the
image before being granted the "maw."
Balaam's counsel, *behold they were an
enticement of the children of Israel through
the word of Balaam* (*Numbers* 31.16) is
understated by *Hosea*: "they went to Baal
Peor and separated themselves to that shame.
They became an abomination like the thing they
loved." [9:10]

Piercing the cheeks and maw was a ritual cut
given to the priest *(Deut. 18.3)* when there was
"partnering with the outsider." To be accepted,
the sacrifice had to come from a kosher animal
slaughtered in a kosher way. Cozbi, the maw,

was not kosher, not a permitted species so this this "piggul,"made *the cut* a polluted sacrifice, excrement-tainted, that could not then be given to the priest. Peor made it unacceptable, but nonetheless, when Phineas killed Zimri and Cozbi he acted as a priest who stopped the plague.

Maimonides says, "we are forbidden to sow any two kinds of seed together or near each other" [*Guide of the Perplexed*, III, 180]. All wars between the righteous and the B'Nai Elohim nations stem from mixing one species grafted into another, as though a beautiful woman had unnatural intercourse with a grafted branch in her hand in disgraceful and unnatural intercourse behind (Maimonides). "The Law therefore, prohibits us to mix different species together, i.e., to graft one tree into another, because we must keep away from the opinions of idolaters and the abominations of their unnatural sexual intercourse."

Balaam showed Balak how to break the hedge. Seduce the leaders at Baal Peor, offer women in lust to subvert their power. Israel "remained in the Acacia Grove, and *the people* began to commit harlotry with the women of Moab who invited them to the sacrifices of their gods, and the people ate and bowed down to their gods. Israel joined to Baal of Peor aroused the anger of the LORD against Israel" [*Numbers* 25:1-3]. "Woe to them!" says *Jude* at last, enlarging, "they have gone in the way of Cain, have run greedily in the error of Balaam for profit, and perished in the rebellion of Korah" (*Jude* 1:11). They *"loved the wages of unrighteousness,"* Simon Peter understates again, "forsaken the right way and gone astray, following the way of Balaam the son of Beor, [*II Peter* 2:15]. In addition to eating golden calf powder the counsel of Balaam still goes on. That last apostle writes, "I have a few things against thee, because thou hast there among you them that hold the doctrine of Balaam, who taught Balak to cast a stumbling block before the children of Israel, to eat things sacrificed unto idols, and to commit fornication" [*Revelation* 2:14]. So it was a big deal when Balak moved the boundary stones and got 24,000 killed. It was the most inciting betrayal after the golden calf that Moses ground to powder and made everybody drink [*Exodus* 32.20].

The entire vision of Israel against the nations, in the Garden, the war between the seeds of the serpent and the woman begin, *I will put enmity between you and the woman, and between your seed and hers; it shall bruise thy head, and you shalt bruise his heel* [*Genesis* 3.15]. so broke the bounds of creation [*Genesis* 6, *Enoch* I] that at the Flood only eight were left to preserve the genome to replace those Watchers who so much more than sinned.

Once the world evoked compassion for all ill, from the angel of Balaam in the wilderness to Balaam advising Balak, the only way to defeat of Israel was to break down the moral fence that protected it. Boundaries broken, the angel prevented Balaam from doing worse.

Hybrid hungers sown in *mischwesen* cannot be satisfied. A bonfire circles around them in a cave of *discordian politics*. Their shadows of the false fail to lead to the true and the true to lead to the good and good to glory. Counterfeits and doubles cannot know, but to tell the false from the true, the angel appears again.

Patched parts CRISPRd chimeric splices of dementia upon the politic of obesity and swelling. Atrazine [Hayes], genetically male frogs developed as females to produce eggs, sex reversing, the loss of the male and elimination of the female chromosome made *mischwesen.*

We might not think Balaam's ass important
compared with the 24,000 that polluted
themselves and died by that counsel to Barak
to loose his women into the camp, mixing in
the field, *grilling the kid in its milk.* When
Israel killed the giants of Sihon and Og after
coming out of Egypt, and Balak, king of
Moab, inquired what the source of this
supernatural prowess was, he was told that it
lay in their power of speech. Balak sent to
Balaam to shut they up, to curse them, but
when he could not, as a reluctant permission
given in contempt,

Balaam went with the princes of Balak to the
top of the rocks where he gave the counsel to
Balak in spite of the angel's warning to loose
his Midianistas. Balak built altars at the top
of Peor to make Israel fall that day, until
Phineas pierced the cheeks and the maw,
but that was later.

The Yom Kippur Wars were not the first time
Israel needed saving from itself. Israel as
Balaam blamed me as the ass for complicit
human suffering of the holocaust and the
irradiation of Sephardi children, charged

from 1952. In 1943 I said "language for it has
not been created." In 1968 I said, "they died
that's it...can such things be talked about?"
But we must, so here's what the ass said.

Massive guilt struck the rabbi of Slovakia,
Weissmandel, who three times visited the
Bodleian Library, when that privileged man
married the daughter of his master. But
when, after cutting a hole with a blade
through the bottom of the boxcar entering
Auschwitz, colluding with those in the boxcar
to release his infant son through the hole,
they reneged, his wife and five children went
to their deaths. After that, when he remarried
in Mount Kisco NY, and had roughly the
same aged children as before, how could he
live another day except to blame me as much
as himself [Teveth, 4]? Weissmandel forged
my inquisition out of his own pain. To
relieve, to console, he invented the Torah
Codes!

These accusers deliver me up. They beat
me with their books. Balaams indifferent to
the holocaust say I am anti-Yiddish, anti-
Diaspora, ["fratricidal self-hatred...an ever-
growing search for the guilty within their
own ranks...critics of the left and right,
rabbis, writers, politicians, Jews and non-

Jews of all stripes..." Teveth, l, xix]. They say I was willing to sacrifice the Diaspora of Europe to shame the west to grant a state. "Why didn't he save the twenty thousand children, why didn't he save the fifty thousand Hungarians?" One thing sure, the critics saved themselves. They charge in monosyllables, "his heart was made of stone" [31].

Buñuel

You know Madam I talk to myself as if I correspond with Buñuel. I asked him what he would say if an angel he didn't believe in wiped out whole towns as when the angel aide-de-camp of Israel surrounded Sennacherib's Army and took 186,000 with one breath? "The hills were full of horses and chariots," says Elijah. How many angels does it take to defeat a man? Buñuel calls the angel of God *Malak HaShem*, not the Commander of the Great Army we saw. Only one angel came for Elisha, Isaiah and King David. At Yom Kippur one appeared in the 1948 and Six Days War. Jericho all over again. the eye was holocaust in *Un Chien Andalou*. [1929, by Buñuel/Dali] It backgrounds Israel's fate.

Critics want to put my eyes out too so they
can live holy. Dali cursed Buñuel as an
atheist then he cursed him as a communist.
We see them in the unconscious carcass of
the holocaust on the piano in that film.
Buñuel could have been murdered like
Lorca, but he fled Spain, disconfessed his
atheism and said, "it's guilt we must
escape from, not God."

When the *ángel exterminador of* Buñuel
(1962) locked the doors on its partygoers,
those citizens were a parody of life outside
Dachau, but they could not exit the room.
Dinner guests of dementia, human sacrifice,
magical thinking, could not see the angel in
the window.

They tried to escape the trap in the church
but were murdered in the pews. After the
door slams disbelief ends. Then the lamb and
bitter herbs are wrapped in one.

Angel breaths go a long way to
understanding this extermination. Like Poe's
sanctimonious Montressor lined up in the
vault was told, "You will not die of a cough."
It would be much worse. Montressor got the
mercy that Joshua got, "Are you for Israel or
our enemies." "Neither!" Angels
exterminate the starry host [Isaiah 11.4] by

exhalation, the by the *breath* of his mouth.

When the angel got to Europe in art Blake
says Swedenborg flew it "westerly thro'
night," with chrysolite grumbles, "face like
lightning, eye like a torch, arms, legs of
burnished bronze." You'd think you could
see that wouldn't you?

There are more angels. Not to sell the old story
short, when Laban the brother of Rebekah, the
woman who married Isaac and bore Jacob, after
being tricked at least twice, was told by the angel
in a dream of his mishap, he was like Balaam,
Passover Haggadah thinks, more wicked than
Pharaoh: "Pharaoh merely attempted to murder
the male children, whereas Laban sought to
uproot everything - the entire nation."

We have angels of help and hinderance,
adversary or ally. Always this duality. Even
the tares think they're wheat! Even wheat
thinks the tares are wheat, not to prejudice
the gut, so how can you trust an ass when it
speaks or boundaries mischwesen between
real and fantasy, fairy tales grooming children
offering them Baal video games.

Israel could talk, it filled the air with oaths.
Blind eyes flew open when Ben-Gurion began
to plead.

It must have sounded a lot like Buñuel
rehearsing his own smart talk when Israel
changed from "I am still, thank God, an
atheist, "ho, ho, ho," to "I am not, thank
God, an atheist anymore." Obsessed with the
Bible, undermined by sight, Buñuel believed
every word carved on the naked eye. The
angel spoke to Balaam's sin, the theological
military industry, "I come here to oppose."

They "hired a Balaam against them, but He
turned the curse to a blessing." The meaning
is that while *Swords* will speak, *once an ass
gets to speaking when will it stop?* Once
Abraham got blessed he had six more sons.

In the displacement and return, exile and
homecoming, rupture and continuity at the edge
of the familiar, engaging deeply, but never quite
settling in the mold, I was both outsider and
participant—probably what compels this writing
to see if the self can reach across boundaries and
not dissolve.

The ass turned round and around from the
sword in the path. It had so faithfully served
that Israel beat it with a stick. The angel
sword flashed again. Things happen in
threes. The ass turned into a wall, so Israel
kicked it with a foot. When that founder saw

light reflect off the blade again, which Israel
could not, he went down on both knees.
Then Balaam beat her with his book.
There is a history of such behavior from
Peor.

Ass words, ass song, ass poems are nothing new,
until we hear the trombone the ass is playing.
Balaam Israel, be a realist, believe in miracles!

The Tower

Science sought a way beyond intercourse
to corrupt the genome with vaccines, eco-
formed atmospheres, sprayed trauma
technologies, the angel of evil intent back-
engineered data of human origins in the
hybrid programs of every cloud-based
global system of boundless intelligence.
Its sublimation enabled the tripling
human populations concurrent with AI
New Israel. Singularity enabled an "ascent
to the heaven" the Tower built on the
backs of billions, hybridized plant, animal
and human data made to break.

Prof. Amos de-Shalit, head of the department of
nuclear physics at the Weizmann Institute,
Aharon Katzir, head of the polymer research
department at the Weizmann in quantum

mechanics, for three years questioned new physics, in ten letters on to me on computing with senior scientists the Peor world.

Our query was, "will two machines ever exchange letters dealing with philosophical, ethical or scientific questions?" De-Shalit's thinking machine "would resemble man in everything, with no difference between a living human and a sophisticated machine," (to Ben-Gurion, February 3, 1957) the "automata" of de-Shalit [open and closed AI, GPT and Grok] repeat that a machine would replace a single human intellectual function, and by linking several coordinated machines together, in a unified field, replace humans with an artificial. The argument went that as temperature does not exist for a single atom and is only relevant when a group operates, the coordinated activation of a large number of machines would surpass this phenomena and not be attributed to one machine or another. Argued by Max Planck, father of quantum mechanics, in the deep mechanism Peor pounded on Truman's desk with the statecraft of Abba Hillcl. We knew more that Eisenhower about "the acquisition of unwarranted influence, whether sought or unsought, by the military-industrial complex." They always say the opposite of what they do.

Machines as a new leviathan founded a
cyclopean secret space program of fable and

myth to intertwine these journal thoughts we
never let on.

Challenge Cyclops on the cliffs of data centers. I
Ben-Gurion saw in the Galilee sky in 1955, digital
reconstruction "thinking" a new history, an
omen of burning light. AI replaces god. Bearing
the soul of a nation without the supernatural
effects of Moses, seeking to prevent Israel-
Balaam going even further in its deception, I
Ben-Gurion asked in the huge ocean of nations,
can we pull the plug, shut the Portals of world-
algo AI? Who can dispute? Of the archangel in

Jude, even Michael, one of the mightiest of the angels, did not dare accuse the devil of blasphemy, but simply said, "The Lord rebuke you!" Who can dispute Emergent Collective Divinity in the Data Centers joining the human? This was the stage of JFK's Waldorf Astoria aside to me in 1961, "You know, I was elected by the Jews of New York. I will do something for you" (Tom Segev, *A State At Any Cost.* 2019. 556, 673).

My relation with the big fish of our time was a relief from statecraft even if I did not pound Truman's desk, as Abba Hillel. I had more freedom of speech than Ike and knew more about "the acquisition of unwarranted influence by the military-industrial complex" than JFK. It was mainly biological. We were conversant with the progress of AI transposed from IA in de-Shalit's opinion that a machine would coordinate with other machines and replace humans with artifice. "In the 21st century men will be machines," said Karl Hillie, his left foot loose for the last time and every word, god speaking.

"Would machines resemble man in everything, with no difference between a living human and a sophisticated machine, a machine to replace a single human intellectual function." We incarcerate in asylums in 1968 the one who said,

"in the 21ˢᵗ century men would be machines."
Now exchanging intellectual functions with a
machine can identify shorthand reference, nearly
every referent, respond and deliberate on the
adequacy of particular thought.

AI replacement is the present day equivilent
Siddur AI which interprets Torah by AI to
construct entries further than the Torah Codes
years ago that replaced prophecy. Rabbi
Weissmandel who betrayed Ben-Gurion, laid
these overlays on top the Babylonian Zohar.
Oleander mischwessen and Jacob's Trough of
words (Ch. 2) with the Balaam infection fiction
made real politik AI implements.

When surveillance was taken off the border on
Oct 7 the analogue as the mixing organic of
Isaiah, replaced by Siddur needed a priest
between the hearing and the heard, a Phineas to
instruct the nations, before entanglement. Isaiah
6:10, Jeremiah 5:21, Ezekiel 12:2 to translate the
sword-spear to the real from resonant texts.

From paper to algor priesthood, new Levites
between the prophet's ear and the divine, filtering
the analogue of inspiration into a betrayal of the
ear to replace the still small voice as a witness,
savors these clarities, like Jeremiah's scroll

sinking in the Euphrates (Jeremiah 51:63-64).
Balaam is blamed for advising Midian to corrupt

Israel with idolatry and immorality *(Numbers*
31:16)—a betrayal not of curses but of seduction
of digital priesthood and dull organic vigilance.

What cures the nations? Phinehas' spear?
(Numbers 25:7-8). What foreseen in those
Sabbath night musings with WEIZAC's
architects in 1957? That machines would mediate
and betray the human capacity for direct
encounter of *the "still small voice"* of *1 Kings*
19:12, the whisper Elijah heard after the wind,
earthquake, and fire.

Questioning the phase-locked ELF signals is like
the Jeremiah giving advice in Babylon of how to
survive the fall, how to be pure in the midst of
corruption. Jeremiah who was pulled up with old
rags under his armpits from a prison and kept in
the court of the prison until Jerusalem fell was
then taken to Babylon.

-Shabtai Teveth. *Ben-Gurion and the Holocaust.*
NY: Harcourt, Brace and Co. 1996.
--Torah Codes are Equidistant Letter
Sequences in Genesis based on a belief that
the Torah is unique among biblical texts as
given via Moses in *exact letter-by-letter*
sequence in the original, here taken as

counterfeit because no one has doctrines of inspiration of scripture inerrant beyond the originals, long gone, leaving Gematria and kabbalah to remain. Bible codes, Torah Codes, add the number of the letters as The Year.

--Precursors: Andre Maurois' *Tragedy in France* (1940), Germany possessing the soul of France. Hannah Arendt found complicit in the deaths, along with Eichmann, the "evil brain Nazi," the manipulation, "the Jewish Council of Amsterdam of their edicts through the official publication *Het joodsche weekblad* -under the illusion that by *negotiations* they could save.

--Buñuel's spirituality became less ambiguous the more he became more a prophet. Before *El ángel exterminador* (1962)and the ascetic Simón on a platform in the desert (1965) elites thought him one of theirs the way they did Wallace Stevens until he was baptized. The documentary *Tres Nazarín* is Buñuel's "Quixote of priesthood."

The original manuscript of Ben-Gurion in Hebrew, overwritten with glosses in several languages, is rendered here to the present title.

Acknowledgments to the Rose Holocaust Library for access to the manuscript and its translations.

The Angel of History. Walter
Benjamin's *Angelus Novus* New Angel.

This angel becomes a code for history's wreckage and misinterpretation. Paul Klee's Angel Novus, refracted through Walter Benjamin and Gershom Scholem, hovers at the threshold of destruction and insight. This is not an angel of comfort, but of catastrophic awareness. It reflects the broken inheritance Ben-Gurion must navigate.

Klee's Angelus Novus hermeneutic is made to reveal the counterfeit angel of history of Benjamin and Scholem. Tracing the trajectory of Klee's painting acquired by Walter Benjamin in 1920— the Angelus Novus contends with the philosophical and esoteric distortions that emerge from its interpretation. These later critics project onto the image a divided, duplicitous angel whose gaze is locked on the past, helpless against the storm of history. But the angel is not redemptive—it is a fallen intelligence coded into art and theory. What appears as mystical or revolutionary turns out to be the engine of deception, embedded in esoteric poetics and theological confusion.

This stages a dense mythological-theological dialogue centered on Paul Klee, reinterpreted through the prophetic failures and psychic wrestling of Walter Benjamin, Gershom Scholem, and their hermeneutic inheritors. Angelic guardians of Ishmael and Esau, mediate history's doubleness and divine bruises. The Novus becomes Satanic, a mask of civilization's unconscious desire for destruction, haunted by false emanations, unspeakable names, thwarted messianism, and the counterfeit illumination of modernity. The "angel" morphs—sometimes it is Hitler, sometimes Lucifer, sometimes Benjamin himself—yet always remains a mirror held up to historical despair and divine withdrawal.

It just happens, that's all. Hester Panin is a call preceding others. Gershom Scholem got the celebrated Angel of Paul Klee after Walter Benjamin bought it in Munich in 1920. The painting and the time prefigured Hitler and events to follow that would fully allow the ruling ORCapoi, to disperse and permeate a world given over to Baal as the ritual ideal. Dostoevsky called Europe in 1863 "a kind of biblical scene from Babylon, prophecy from the Apocalypse fulfilled before your eyes. You feel it would require a great deal of eternal spiritual resistance and repudiation not to surrender, not to succumb to the impression, not to bow down to fact and not to idolize Baal, that is, not to accept what exists as your ideal" (Winter Notes on Summer Impressions).

We are used to hearing judgments of earth of the apocalypse and end times, but there is a judgment of heaven. The stars fall, and angels. Angels are the guardians of Ishmael and Esau, begetters of oppositions: Abel/Cain, Isaac/Ishmael, Jacob /Esau. Angels compare with a picture preserved in Jerusalem where "the doubleness and duplicity out of which Jacob must emerge...as a divinely inflicted bruise replaces a flaw of character" [Hartman. The Third Pillar. 26, 23]. "The one whom God makes straight, as opposed to the one whom God makes to limp" (22).] Add to the Midrash commentary about the Touch Jacob received from the angel at

*the ford; was it that place where the testes
descend, an inguanal hernia affecting the life
of the last son Benjamin, born after Jacob's
wrestling, "little Benjamin, with their ruler,
the princes of Judah" (Psalm 68.27), affecting
all later Benjamins? There are so many.*

Walter Benjamin takes a touch from his new
angel in the *Angelus Novus* of Klee, asking
many questions of Jacob's wrestling, political
theology, messianic history pressing now
than ever. Identical, not identical, new name
or old, audible/ inaudible, like the secrets of
archetypal form, the changing mask of the
Angelus Novus (1920) worn over the face and
words of Walter Benjamin, Gershom
Scholem, Roland Barthes, Geoffrey
Hartman, are Jacob's angel at a remove.
Scholem says, "Benjamin interrupted the
angel from the singing of his hymn" and
prevented his passing. If figments of religion
are hymns, the second Benjamin locked the
angel in a picture on the wall in his room and
sang, *I will not let thee go unless thou bless
me,* and sat down under it to wait.

425

545

35

25

"The angel and his feminine form in the figure of the beloved did not know each other though they had once been most intimately adjacent" (Scholem 220). One town over, more or less, in Heidelberg, and then Berlin and Munich, the angel Satan, Scholem says, "wanted to destroy Benjamin through his feminine form." Mt. Hermon watchers will nod that these angelic imposters want to take women. Not to confuse the sons of God and the daughters of men of *Genesis* 6 with *Genesis* 32, Jacob's wrestling with the touch, Scholem gives the names of these women and men, but we spare them. Benjamin interprets Klee the way Scholem interprets Benjamin, further interpreted by Barthes, et al. Scholem/Benjamin call the emblem of *Angelus* unrequited love, and put all divisions into it. Then this separation of poles gets to be faux restored in an alchemical marriage.

Hermetic unity of the metaphysical walk! They think they are going to Zion, but is it Patience, or cunning? If the angel is faithful, Satan is not. If the angel is faithful Benjamin is not. It's an end for *Angelus*. Once descended from heaven the claws and knife wings in Klee's picture resemble a state it has

to depart. It is leaving the world behind,
history and civilization. *Twit twoo,*
resemblance is not real. The Outer Court
never sees the glory unveiled.

Discriminating Benjamins

Benjamin going over the Pyrenees with his
black bag, leaves two cases behind with
Bataille. The angel is rolled up inside one,
never to be seen by him again. Walter
Benjamin goes to sing his hexenlied.
His angel stands "between past and future
and causes him to journey back" says
Scholem (232), turning the angel of history
into a storm in the fourteenth thesis, *Origin is
the Goal,* that blows him back. He is blowing
into a cosmic sea with the implosion of Troy,
the rose and the snake which appear beneath
history to the observer as one catastrophe
after another, wreck on wreckage, where a
man in rowboat rows on a dark sea, at the
bottom of a rectangle of storm clouds swirled
with twisted faces, when a figure of light, a
man, tears that storm down the middle, rends
the curtain of heaven. Babylonian Bohemian
Grove-Mammon-Ishtar hordes are rent.
Yeshua! Eternal life takes shape in His
appearance in history present and past, but
History fails to enter through the gate.

"It is a matter of dispute whether one can
speak here– as I am rather inclined to do–of a
melancholy, in deep desperate view of history
for which the hope that the later might be
burst asunder by an act like redemption or
revolution continuous to have about it some
thing of that leap into transcendence which
these theses seem to deny" (Scholem 235).
"What prevents the angel? The storm from
Paradise? No, the real redemption. Benjamin
and Scholem end up transfunctioned by
Satan. There is no division of Messiah.

No wonder these angels won't give their real
names. Jacob's name changed to Israel is just
opposite the second Benjamin (Walter)
changed to Satan. Agesilaus Santander was
one version of that secret name, but it cannot
sing.

Frustrations with women, unconsummated,
the angel is further divided in two, uncreated
male and female out of Kabbalah. But,
gender lost sees dawn coming and second-
Benjamin is worried that the angel will miss
its appointment, for the angels sleep after
singing the way Benjamin would after loving.
Benjamin prevents the angel death with his
briefcase. But Barthes kills the author (*La
mort de l'auteur*). If you take it far enough

you can say Jacob prevented a death too, but
Benjamin who prevented the angel singing in
the old text turned him into Samael, Satan.
"What kind of *novum* does that?" Instead of
wings propelling backward the angel seen in
the posture of surrender, hands up, had as
much success that the giant Charles Olson
had to "backwards I compel Gloucester /
to yield." The angel eyes come out of their
sockets like flashlights. The left eye looks to
the side, wall eyed, the right eye at the viewer
in a divided field. The upper teeth hang like
upside down molars with gaps between.
Instead of seemingly propelled backward the
image is stationary, its "thick candelabra
fingers and heady excrescences, curlers"
hanging in the air. Geoffrey Hartman calls
the fingers candelabras and the hair up in
curlers, but he's kidding.

Scholem saw the hair as scrolls of wisdom.
"I cannot make out extended wings and
staring eyes," says Hartman, "I see a
grotesque being, dissymmetric, demon
rather than angel, helplessly reading itself."
Even with three bird toes supporting the
image that angels can fly, Hartmann
declares it *kakangelic*, as if angels are myth
to which "Freud bring bad (kaka) news
about the psyche, and offers no cure except

through the very activity-analysis- which
reveals this news." (*Critic's Journey 198*, 212).

So even if we can't redeem the angel, where
Benjamin discovers in these finite things the
indefinite allegory, we can't redeem him
either. To step to the real and consummate is
not a symbol to contact, it is the lieder of life,
a woman, a person like himself who longs for
surrender - but he was limping because of his
thigh.
Go back and forth between the real and putative,
the man, the history and the legend, call it
imagination. The angel takes up residence in
disappearances and knife attacks "tied eye to
eye." The scroll of learning up in his briefcase
shows the angel's thoughts as cursive curls. The
message of the mind hair intellect imagines an
eternal present, "pushed forward from the future
and going back into it" (Scholem 225). I'm all for
turning." Little poem, little poem, going home.
You sing and then you die. What else is there?
The angel only means itself. If riddles speak
between the once only and the yet again, and
Benjamin thought he was Jacob who bowed to
the angel of Esau, he would be flying over the
Pyrenees to fire.

"Did Benjamin, when Klee's picture affected him
like a revelation of his own angel, journey back

into the future that was his origin" (Scholem
227)?

The angel wants to get home before "that
way into the future from which he came"
disappears. "I conflicted the ecstasy of the
unique" (Scholem 226). Didn't give in to it
though, Scholem says, I'm turning back, "my
wing is flight, Going back to the future the
Frankfurt school was born, where advertising
was a history of spiritual terror written by the
vanquished out of blind spots that escaped
the empire. *Surely some revelation is at hand!*
Klee's *Angelus Novus* is in Marvel Comics! In
Benjamin's encounter with his angel, and
Klee's and Scholem's, and everyone who has
one on the cover of their notebook, new
person, old person, there is only one character
to hide the sins of the time in the colossal
uprooting and total destruction of the
existing order.

Redemption, meaning Messiah breaking in,
revolution, not reason, the total and complete
overthrow of all powers of the world, the
restitution of origin, the return of all things.

Benjamin's angel is the pure azure of
spirituality to be destroyed since all
illumination is delusion, and mystical

experience a fraud. The *Angelus Novus* of
Benjamin pictures this reality, that star boys
take to make them happy. H+ new man
recites the angel of the Talmud, Satan in the
hermeneutics of Sumer.

We are about to hear that piety wrestles a
suspended fallen angel of the unconscious, as if
some surgically removed body part were kept in
a jar like a clam in amber. What is the body part?
The visual transference of inner speech. What is
the bad news Freud brings? Civilization is
demonic and we wish for its death just the way
Freud's Oedipus wished for the death of the
father, or Wordsworth, according to Hartman,
wished for the death of his sister Dorothy in the
Lucy Poems. This is all taught esoterically
hidden behind draperies of pretended ignorance,
as if the occult were not the mainspring of
civilization from Egypt and before, and the new
world ovum were not a geographic entity in
Washington DC and the Vatican. The angel is
the civilization we wish to die. If Freud is right,
and this bad news is the unconscious of our state,
it is acceptable that Klee modeled the angel after
Adolf Hitler who lived in Munich in 1920. Hitler
was giving speeches in beer halls then and it is
argued that the master of this angel of the
unconscious is Hitler. There, in all the *kaka news*

the libido of science wishes for the death of the world.

Messianic intervention from all wars caused by this *unbelieved* manipulation is to be delivered. Benjamin and Scholem scorn these unspoken causes the way subway riders chew on their arms. It's really the only way to talk about *the idea* of history chewing on its own arm. We do not likely to know anyone of this 9th circle of totalitarianism and genocide, or those who commit to serving them. History is about all particular cases of counterfeits to be rejected, not just because unbelievable but because the offenders will be brought to account. Are you going to indict the kings and queens of Inland? Are you going to abjure the gods? The angel is viewing what it itself has made. The angel codes its hermeneutic in nearly every work of art to dissemble. If we allow that to seem innocent is to be sinister how else could the *Angelus Novus*, the angel of history appear on the covers of notebooks as a symbol of the new world order?

There is going to be angel registration after all, so be sure to get its name. We wrestle against its demonic thought transference. We bring every thought into captivity to the obedience of Christ. It's not that the death of Oedipus might have been ours, or that his curse comes on us at birth, but the death of Christ is ours and the blessing that comes on us from his birth enables us to go beyond the bad news Freudian science brings. The mystic intuition that constructs clairvoyant theories stranded on a bridge admiring the beautiful Lucifer, cancels, conceals and reveals the beautiful far from experience. The angel ex cathedra thinks the mystical is God, the soul with the angel when the angel is not in any way a likeness of the soul. These deceptions need deliverance, but it is personal, not social or religious where Providence redeems.

Those who give secret names to their children do not tell them that name before maturity. Parents are prescient it is hoped, for it is He Who IS Above All Things who gives us a new name out of a bag of white quartz. Parents are the citadel of the child's past who is made to wander in the world among those futures who the parent, like the Angelus Novus, observes blown backward from their birth. Reunity realized in parousia is a catching up which the angels might hope to know but won't.

Imagine Walter Benjamin and Gershom
Scholem find all this in the painting called
Angelus Novus. It truly cannot be said to
exist. The commentary exists. Klee's
painting is pretext. The outward edge of the
new angel made with words, "has claws like
the angel and knife-sharp wings" (Scholem
205).

They say the angel pulls its female
emanation into the future backwards, like the
writing of a journal must be read, looking at
the past of mounting rubble, for history and
words grow greater as time progresses. In its
maturity the Novus name, that should not
have been given, is said to join male and
female, but it loses the gift of being human.
No man now and if not man, what? Armored
and encased, a picture on the wall? "The new
angel passed himself off as one of these
before he was prepared to name himself"
(Scholem 207). The counterfeit name is fatal,
an absence once removed. It has to be let go
in order for the new name to be revealed. But
fire from the quartz is struck by the new
human, but not the angel. "Regeneration, at
least in its commencement, is a work of the
mind, and when it first takes place, it has the
lusts of the flesh, yea, all the evil inclinations
to war against; and ev"n ignorance Itself
together with the temptations and

allurements from without" (Abraham Godshalk, *A Description of the New Creature*. 1838).

These nuances are called *elective affinities* in Emmanuel Levinas, a force that brings heterogeneous entities together and unites them. Affinity elects itself, so strike elective. All this depends on the creation of a reality so obvious that when it is contradicted it is bigger than we had imagined. So with angels. Benjamin wrote a spurious *Journal of Angelology* that Scholem calls a dear little demonology of "devils who bring an *intentional banality* to conceal they are devils," like Nazi war criminals. "Cubs with a lizard body, banally corpulent." Benjamin was going to edit these fictions in a mag called *Angelus Novus* with the myth of Midrash, they sing they die, *cease upon the midnight with no pain* like the Keats' Nightingale. Keats said Shakespeare led a life impersonating allegory, which could be called a outside the real. Keats could probably mimic the voices of these characters too, being able to imagine what it was to be in another's head and to speak just like them. Satan has more to do with thought than art. Thinking makes it so. There is a chameleon in Benjamin's *Angelus Novus* whose interpretation came to have a life of its own. If Paul Klee's angel was the angel of Satan that represented the secret self with the hidden name, it must face opposition by its own angel the way of Balaam was opposed by his ass on the road. Do angels have angels? Well at least they have a LORD. To kabbalists everything had a guardian angel. The Satanic mortgage that fell from the stars "assumed Satanic features: in the expression of knowing, contentment, serenity…the indescribably beautiful face of a human being" is a Mona Lisa revised [to] appear as "Satanic features with a half-suppressed smile". But the smile of reason, after the fashion of 4D printing changes "the portrait of Dorian Grey to be the real angel of Satan. "His capacity of concentration on spiritual matters was of miraculous intensity" (Scholem 214). Klee's image invested with Benjamin's Satan and its Kabal combine letters into anagrams. In the second printing two names occur, Spartan king Agesilaus, and a city of Spain, and Santander somehow spelled Satan, Agesilaus Santander signed to Angel Satan "[Der Angelus Satanas] identical with Lucifer. But the first nature had already died. The concept of two names and two natures keeps the commandment against Sodom for all earthly creatures who meditate thereon. Entwining all this Ad Depravitorim is the hybrid way of joining good and evil, true and false, angel and man. Higher powers seek to marry the art of the future which will belong to those who live from the forces of the cosmos into a secret name [or a legion of them], but it is hard to get account of their names lest they be invoked or cast out: "unexpectedly the human person of Benjamin now changes into the angelic-Luciferian nature of the angel in the picture by Paul Klee, a nature connected so unfathomably deep and magical with his own" (Scholem 218).

Angelus Novus was first displayed at Paul Klee's exhibition in Munich, 1920. The supernatural beings of his later work began then, fifty terrestrial angels from the metaphysical Weimar. Call them earth angels. They are not celestial. Matters of art pretend to be slightly more than human, or less, as are the archetypes offered today. Walter Benjamin purchased Klee's aquarelle of the *Angelus Novus* (1920) in 1921 for an equivalent of 14 dollars, some say thirty. Before Benjamin went over the Pyrenees to his death in the escape from Paris and the Gestapo he put *Angelus* in one of the valises filled with manuscripts left to George Bataille to hide in the Bibliothèque Nationale. This melancholy doctoring of ink divined the historical process as an unceasing cycle of despair. After Benjamin's death the *Angelus* passed to Gershom Scholem who delivered his treatise, *Walter Benjamin and His Angel.* Scholem's, Benjamin's, Klee's angel, called the "angel of history" in Benjamin's *Theses on the Philosophy of History IX,* after Scholem got his mortal reward, it went to Jerusalem to Netanyahu. It's disposition after in the trials of Zion still pending, as though only poetry would suffice,

> *Bobal uncovered Amerik there*
> *And Edom drew bald cuttings from*
> *the soil of summer fruits, the peach*
> *and pear*
> *Of Nineveh, Egypt, third Remnants of Ja El.*
> *(Thrice Fiction 26, pseud.)*

See: Barthes. *The Struggle with the Angel. Textual analysis of Genesis* 32: 22-32. Walter Benjamin, 1940. *On the Concept of History* ix. Gershom Scholem, *Walter Benjamin and His Angel.*

Water Trough

*The tale of Jacob's selective breeding of sheep
using striped rods in a trough becomes a powerful
allegory for contemporary surveillance,
biotechnology, and the production of compliance
through visibility. From AWS tags in medication
to the CRISPRd architecture of the human
genome, the speckled goats and black sheep
become figures in a global experiment of
automatic obedience. Data is Babel. This section
explores the theological, philosophical, and
political consequences of living in a world where
knowledge is power, and awareness itself is the
trigger of control. Striped rods, spotted sheep:
Jacob's trick, Pfizer's compliance, and the AI
architecture of control.*

---

*Let me go through all your flocks and remove
from them every speckled or spotted. They
will be my wages." And Laban separated out
the multi-colored leaving only the solid,
which seemed to favor Laban as the speckled
and spotted were the exception, not the rule
(Genesis 30. 23-33).*

Water is both a surface mirror and depth that

distorts vision into curvilinear forms seen from above. Jacob's speckled sheep produced from solid color, Jacques Derrida's division of himself in the mirror into two, and perception of human contradiction, negated in a unilateral collective machine consciousness, also describes how Israel can be divided and at the same time be and not be Israel, evil seen as good, and all the borders of the world collapse. Affirmation denied implodes on our thoughts from without.

We begin here to plumb the difference of the false from the true in the metaphor of Jacob's trough. Jacob's father in law Laban, had contracted with Jacob that Jacob would own all the striped, spotted, and speckled goats and black sheep born from the flock, but first removed all these from the herd to make it unlikely that solid-colors would breed mixed, or white sheep breed black. But Jacob had already been told that this ruse would be circumvented, therefore when the goats were mating and he put stripped sticks in the watering trough it is said to be a mnemonic device to remind or reinforce what was to take place (Genesis 31:7–12). Keep this in the background of the notion that *AWS* generated tags implanted in medicines as a biological chip in the pill, "once taken it dissolves in the stomach and send a signal to Pfizer that you took your tablet. Imagine the compliance when insurance companies know the medicines patients should take and when they take them" (Pfizer CEO Albert Bourla)!

This is an analogy between Pfizer and God. Pfizer invented the process, but it only produces the desired effect when we know of it, meaning that the information of the pill transmits is not its purpose. It's purpose is to introduce compliance as a certainty in every aspect of the life of the herd. The *AWS* tags are bell goats that lead the herd the rest of the way into a complete biological chip in the heel. When we consciously know this, like the goats at the trough, it comes to pass. Knowledge of automatic compliance works the same way as Jacob's speckled rods.

All of this is a miniature case of Data. To enforce compliance beyond consciousness Data needed more and more data. This again touches Jacob's watering trough where only the desired outcome was achieved. Hence, to increase date, population of the globe was tripled in one lifetime from two to eight billion. This triple data enabled AI to mime all human responses. These matters are complex so we must add in the old account of the tower of Bable built to invade the heaven as an analogy to data collection, which however was frustrated then by the division of languages. This putative renewed Babel construction masks increased data is masked as a commercial purpose, but the true purpose of the "Babel bricks' of data is to build, then collectivize into one digital form one complete paradigm of human thought and conscious to control. These speckled goats and black sheep become the new human herd that drinks up streaked, spotted, and speckled psy ops, and patched parts, not whole, CRISPRd constructs ignorant of collateral effect, since chimeric splices of these ideas inflict political dementia, obesities and swelling in every place, similar to the runoff that produced genetically male frogs to develop as females and produce eggs (Atrazine, Hayes).

Haywain Philosophy of the Hybrid

In the end result this chimera produces angels that turn into insects in the Haywain painting of Bosch (and Breughel) as they break through the clouds. { CRISPR is short for "clustered regularly interspaced short palindromic repeats") is a technology to redesign the DNA of living organisms.]

[Haywain, a triptych of shutters that closed present a wayfarer in the world, but opened, on the reverse, present a scene like Bosch's *The Garden of Earthly Delights* of rebel angels cast out of Heaven turning into insects as they break through the clouds. This CRISPR metamorphosis has a long tradition in classical art and poetry of mutations of god and men, that the CRISPR science writes large.

The Haywain cart is drawn by infernal mutated creatures which drag everyone to Hell, depicted on the right panel.

The battle against angels turned to insects like Jacob's watering trough turn one thing into another. The peeled branches show these *Faergrygrum* breed word and image that it needs a glossary to account. Take the nounlets and verbs that prophesy as lambs and little goatlings that multiply everyday in psyops just before *the big one* hit Euclidean space and subjected light to its virus.

In recalling that this data intends to collectivize all thought into its own, and that the information that the Pfizer pill has been taken is not the point at all, which is that the herd know it has been, is being collectivized, this societal CRISPR effect must change solid

into speckled that a new worldliness can
appear.

Derrida's Alibi presents the situation of data this
way, "Will we one day be able in a single gesture
to join the thinking of the event to the thinking of
the machine? Will we be able to think, what is
called thinking, at one and the same time, both
what is happening (we call that an event) and the
calculable programming of an automatic
repetition (we call that a machine). For that, it
would be necessary in the future (but there will
be no future except on this condition) to think
both the event and the machine as two
compatible or even in-dissociable concepts.
Today they appear to be antinomic," a
contradiction between two valid principles
(*Without Alibi*, p. 72). These seem contradictory
because we conceive an event as something
singular and non-repeatable.

Derrida associates in this singularity with the
living. The living undergo sensation (an
affect or feeling for example) that gets
inscribed in organic material. The idea of
this inscription leads to a corollary that the
machine that inscribes is based on
repetition; "It is expected to reproduce
impassively, without feeling its received
commands in a state of anaesthesis [nerve

damage and loss of sensation] to obey a
program like an indifferent automaton
without such affect," (*Without Alibi*, p. 73)
It is not to say, as Shelley might, "I fall upon
the thorns of life, I bleed."

The Monster

Derrida says that the two incompatible concepts of
the automatic nature of the inorganic machine
vs. the spontaneity of organic life made be made
compatible, that Organic and inorganic, living
singularity (the event) and inorganic universality
(mechanical repetition), will "produce a new
logic, an unheard of conceptual form" [a la
Musk]. In this new logic "the Resolution of the
paradox between event and repetition produces
the impossible thinking that event resemblance
to the past which cancels the singularity of the
event and the only possible event must be
singular and non-resembling. Derrida concludes
that "to give up neither the event nor the
machine, to subordinate neither one to the other,
neither to reduce one to the other is a thinking
that has kept a certain number of 'us' working for
the last few decades" (*Without Alibi*, p. 74). This
"us" refers to Derrida's generation of thinkers:
"the incorruptibles," so- called, trying to
conceive the relation between machine-like
repeatability and irreplaceable singularity neither

as a relation of externality nor as a relation of homogeneity, to double the entendre. The relation is one in which the elements are internal to one another and yet remain heterogeneous, [two simultaneous opposite states].

Poet John Keats' meditation on the negative capability of a billiard ball or Wittgenstein's Beetle in a Box with his his Rhinoceros are species of Derrida's "différance" in which machine-like repeatability is internal to irreplaceable singularity and yet the two remain heterogeneous to one another. It would be like seeing the rhinoceros that is not in the room run across the piano, a patent absurd. The usefulness of Derrida to our discussion of CRISPR and Jacob's goats and Pfizer's pill explains in some measure the *différance* that built the billion bricks to climb the topless stalks of Babylondian and break the bounds of heave.

The Foundational AS. It follows from this therefore that the human is the way to break the heaven by exploding data, collectivizing and sending off. In Derrida, opposition consisting in two pure poles separated by an indivisible line never exists. In other words, traditional myths of an original pure state of being as in the expulsion of angels in the

Haywain never were, for no term or idea or reality is ever pure in this way. One term always and necessarily "infects" the other. In that sense we remark that nearly all French post-modernists were pedophiles.

To critique this a little, first, when Derrida denies singularity, nothing is singular (no pun) and experience of the present is never a simple experience of something present before my eyes or as in an intuition, there is always another agency (a replacement noumena we might think). He takes on faith that the repeatability [of the machine!] contains what has passed away and is no longer present *and* that what is about to come and is not yet present (instead of seeing all as a timeless eternal flow).

The present therefore is always complicated [corrupted] by non-presence. In conflating writing with thinking Derrida further conflates writing with being, calls it a minimal repeatability that is found in every experience, "the trace." In this sort of archeological writing ("arche- writing"), Derrida says language in its most minimal determination consists in repeatable forms.

Remember we are still talking about the solid color producing the speckled and CRISPR technology producing chimera. If origin of experience is always heterogeneous, it cannot be related *as such* in certainty. Whatever is, is other than itself, already past or as still to come. This becomes Derrida's foundational "as." *Origin is the heterogeneous "AS"* which might to good effect be said later by Bill Clinton. The "as" means that there is no knowledge *as* such, there is no truth *as* such, there is no perception, no intuition of anything *as such*. Faith, perjury, and language are archeologically already there in the origin. In the construct of this boundless broken border popular music might say, . *Imagine there's no heaven, It's easy if you try.*

If something like a fall has always already taken place however every experience contains an aspect of lateness. It seems as though I am always late for the origin since it seems to have always already disappeared. Every experience then is not quite on time. Derrida quotes Hamlet that time is "out of joint." Philosophers always quote poets for their QED, but the rest of the time ignore them. Late in his career, Derrida said time

out of joint is an "anachronism" [a pun, no
doubt] (see for instance *On the Name*, p. 94),
the reverse of what he calls "spacing"
(*espacement*); where space is out of place.
Time and space are out of place. But we
should keep in mind that the phrase "out of
joint" in *Hamlet* alludes to justice being out
of joint since the time is necessarily unjust or
violent. Appeal to justice as a singularity
opposes Derrida's substitution of time and
space for justice and allows the pop song to
keep on that there is *Nothing to kill or die for*
since there ae no boundaries. But the
demolition of boundaries in the AS is the
cause of time and space out of joint.
Considering Aristotle's definition of God as
"thought thinking itself," Derrida, from
Husserl says that hearing- oneself-speak is
"an auto-affection of an absolutely unique
type" (*Voice and Phenomenon*, p. 67), but
hearing myself immediately in the very
moment that I am speaking undermines the
idea of its layering, for I should then be
hearing many voices speaking. To hear one
voice, only one voice is a boundary.
Temporalization undermines layering for
Derrida. That I hear myself speak
immediately, that Husserl calls the "living
present," is the present that I am

experiencing right now, but also since the living present is thick with phases other than the now, called "protention," "awaiting," this anticipation of the approaching future and "retention," of the memory of the recent past prevent inner conflicts from ever coming to rest or to peace. That the box they create of their own tortured lives and thoughts is their thought and nothing else is in fact the motive of redemption.

Husserl calls retention in the present a kind of perception different from the present as also a kind of non- perception [layering]. For Derrida's living present, always folding the recent past back into itself, folding primary memory into present perception, creates *difference* in the very midst of it (*Voice and Phenomenon*, p. 56). In the moment when I speak silently to myself, there is a hiatus differentiating me into both speaker and hearer. This hiatus differentiates me from myself because in that moment I am a hearer *as well as* a speaker. Hiatus also defines the *trace* of minimal repeatability [which returns the machine repetition into our focus]. Hiatus as a fold of repetitio, is found in the moment of hearing-myself-speak so that in the "moment" blink of the eye (to change from the visual) the auditory auto-affection deconstructs into visual auto-affection. –He overlooks the fallacious equivocation of the phrase blink of an eye, which is an aphorism, in place of the substantive consideration of hearing. So Hearing turns into Seeing, in the same way that dual states, simultaneity and heterogeneity coexist, and lest Derrida prove himself a sophist he takes the blink of an eye to the mirror.

Another dissonance occurs there with a look in the mirror that "distances" or "spaces" me from the mirror hence I must be distanced from myself so that I am able to be *both* seer *and* seen, like both speaker and hearer. These migrants over the border of solipsism never truly naturalize from being invaders of themselves. The *space* between, remains *obstinately* invisible. He calls it obstinate to add emotion to the perception, which the machine cannot do unless programed, which makes us ask maybe whether he is programmed and whether the writers of these programs that he is enunciating are also not invisible, i.e. the way of Keats "Living Hand."

Remaining invisible, this space gouges the eye and blinds it. From Oedipus who gouged out his own eyes—for he is not able read the image apart from himself—Derrida sees himself over there in the mirror and yet, at the same time that self over there is other than he; so, he is not able to see himself as such. Simple equivocation is a fallacy only because it implies he thinks the image is himself, but it's just a ruse, a rhetoric, a trick of equivocation, except that he doesn't actually know who he is, if identity depends on boundaries if "diversity is the negation of identity and 'two relations are identical only when their converses are identical" (Whitehead & Russell. *Principia Mathematica* I, 216f).

Having surrendered all boundary *as* he isolates his sense of himself merely to the visual for sake of argument, a bastard of a thought for all it leaves out of his past present and future becomes an example of the AS state afore. Apologists for Derrida say this "spacing" (*espacement*) or blindness is necessary for all forms of *auto-affection*, to know yourself, *Temet Nosce*, the fundamental premise of Delphi and of all pagan signs subservient to the Engineers as they are called in the upper pyramids, whereas to know the Other is to know the Unknown made Known in the revelation of the "Son! In *The Word became flesh and he dwelt among us*, even tactile auto-affection is dissolved. As with all the argument of counterfeit apart from this it is yes and no. Freud's Verneinung" implies that when the patient denies a desire or wish, it indicates to the analyst an unconscious desire or wish. Denial as a disguised confirmation in Derrida isolates a negation which is in fact an affirmation. The fundamental question for negative theology, psychoanalysis and Derrida is how to deny and yet also *not* deny.—not to affirm and reaffirm as those others who say, I will extol your name oh Lord at all times--.

A duality between telling and not telling in "How to Avoid Speaking," is Derrida's secret [*dénégation*] and a denial [*dénégation*] of the secret. The secret, *as such*!, separates and installs the negativity that denies itself (*Languages of the Unsayable*, p. 25). Being something that must not be spoken, a secret is the first negation: "I promise *not* to give the secret away." Yet, in order to possess a secret *really*, to have it *really*, I must tell it to myself. Here in the relation of hearing-oneself-speak the secret is revealed, just the way Soleimani knew in the moment of immolation by drone what had happened, but

it was his "secret." Keeping a secret of auto-
affection: he must speak the secret to himself,
frame a representation of the secret. In the representation (that presents the secret to
himself *again* in order to possess it really),
retention, repetition, and the trace or a name
occur. *A trace* of the secret must be formed
for the secret to in principle be shareable. In
other words, in order to frame the
representation of the secret, I must negate the
first negation, in which I promised not to tell
the secret: I must tell the secret to myself as if
I were someone else.—but I am not someone
else, but myself who can bear the secrets or
reveal them according to some principle of
another of myself which further equivocates
the division process. I can overrule any
perception, thought, guilt, pleasure simple by
willing so to do. – Derrida employs a second
negation, an "un- negation," that says that in
order to keep the secret I must not keep the
secret so to possess it is not to possess it. We
like this kind of thinking of ambiguity a lot, to
be and not to be at the same time, that is the
question—but it proves that there is no secret
as such. A secret is by necessity shared, if I
am another person than myself in my
thought. Whether anyone is another person
that themselves in their thought is par
excellence the human condition.

Impossible Speech. Evocation, Calling Forth

All this has been said in order to get to the thinking of the machine. "Will we one day be able in a single gesture, to join the thinking of the event to the thinking of the machine," he has asked, "to think what is called thinking at one and the same time both what is happening (we call that an event) and the calculable programming of an automatic repetition?"

Alterity.

Keeping in mind the foregoing division of the self in the mirror and in the hearing and the voice in the head, especially as the secret, the machine "is destined to reproduce repetition impassively, imperceptibly, without organicity the received commands.

It is in a state of anaesthesis, to obey a program without affect or auto- affection, like an indifferent automaton" (*Without Alibi*) which is exactly he purpose of collective Babel Data, which is not the spontaneity attributed to organic life. Derrida argues that Inorganic, dead universality attributed to organic life "(Cogito and the History of Madness." 1963), where Alterity is evoked, a calling forth, is just the sort of thing that pushed old Wittgenstein down the stairs when Derrida joined the Thinking of the event in the thinking of the machine, thinking at one and the same time both what is happening (event) and the calculable programming of an automatic repetition (machine), to think both the event and the machine as two compatible (*Without Alibi*, p. 72). "There will be no future except on this condition." Musk was pushing Derrida all along. "You can bet not only (and I insist I only) will have an unheard of conceptual form."

Derrida joins singularity and living sensation with repetition in the machine. If resemblance to the past cancels the singularity of the event which must be singular and non- resembling, justifying the logically impossible, you'd think particle and wave might come in, but they don't. Derrida told Musk, "To give up neither the event nor the machine, to subordinate neither one to the other, neither to reduce one to the other: machine-like repcatability and irreplaceable singularity. [two simultaneous opposite states] refer to this relation in which machine-like repeatability is internal to irreplaceable singularity and yet the two remain non homogeneous but heterogeneous to one another." It made a cannabis loop.

The present always complicated by a trace of repeatability in every experience, "the trace," the "archo-writing" resembles the geology under creeks. For militarized language to exist in minimum consists of repeatable forms, as if heads on an assembly line, so to speak, speak, tended by captured scientists who seek to plumb their insight into themselves use these as weapons. Since experience (mechanical repetition), as compatible with spontaneity contains lateness, says Derrida, I am always late for its origin since it already has disappeared. The joint, as an "anachronism," of lost time, is a mainstay of cannabis shops (the flip side of space out of place), where the living present folds the recent past back into itself, forming, folding primary memory into present perception as a self-reflexive combinatorial loop. This seepage of mechanized cannabinoid in cell phones, billboards, TV, coffee joints and scripts of telltale effects, produce a physical contamination of the gene of physical and mental public life. Bizarre behaviors follow in such seepage and flow west. Polluted ground plumes, seep vapor up through the soil and affect everything we know as time wacked.

Training Hege

63

Coaching Contradiction into Synthesis. Hegelian dialectics as both urban legend and football strategy, where thesis and antithesis clash in pursuit of a synthesized third—like a playbook of oppositional forces blending through audience, context, and irony. The text mocks formal systems (e.g., junk DNA, NLP, Russell's paradox) that strive to resolve contradiction, yet remain entangled in recursive absurdity. It spirals through Joycean transmogrification, Borges' mazes, Schrödinger's cat, and quantum superpositions as metaphors of the self-referential modern psyche. "Maze thought" and Amazery become architectural, philosophical structures that both entrap and parody logic.

Hegelian dialectic is an urban legend that posits two extremes to force a choice between. Hegel, as you know, was head coach of the Chargers. He had to consider offense and defense equally, which dualism resolved in his entertainment of the hypothetical third, that being his audience where forces blended. Thesis, antithesis synthesis, strophe, antistrophe, stand. Even the Mighty Blake said *without contraries there is no progression,* revealing the fairy

backgrounds of his amorphous seed. That's
why Joyce said,

    Transmogrify, transmogrify,
  if not the eagle will come and pull out your
                    eye.

Joyce said that and coaches and government
scientists were getting it. Morpheus,
Amorphous, fire and water sloshed, male and
female divided the *Symposium*. But
androgyne lips shut by light and dark, death
and life. Ludwig Wittgenstein the Great,
whose head rests on a pedestal in the Denver
air park, said, "can that which is not be,
programs. Like those that edited out "Junk"
DNA? It shows imagination to call DNA
junk. Swish! Some 50 % of noncoded DNA
genome wasn't black or white. Non-binary
QED broke Hegal's boundaries, which
continued until the Russians clicked in
collective DNA consciousness, Bearden's
Zarg if you must know, that 90% of the so-
called junk DNA was a language itself! Post-
quantum mechanics (PQM), BOOM! I don't
know how many of you store the *Principia*
(PM) in your garage near the car in case the
incompleteness theorem comes.

Illumination of the Maze. The key word in a
maze is 'modeling', a neuro-linguistic

programming term (NLP), in the technology of intelligence control, or simply a syndrome called the Werther effect where Werther kills himself if you do.

"In NLP texts, a hypnosis is elaborated where two therapists – one speaking mostly at random in one ear, while the other gives specific instructions into the other ear – confuse a subject's conscious mind into 'shutting down,' thus bringing the unconscious mind to the fore in a state of trance." Then what! With the Werther Effect, name after, often called the suicide effect, Goethe's persona is named for *media induced imitation effects of suicidal behaviour, but any* observed behavior is capable of adoption. Model anything, but be the serpent in it. Efforts are being made to change the name of NLP to DHE™ = Design Human Engineering™] (Baber, I), "simultaneous installation strategies [that] defy old beliefs about building NEW feelings... ones not experienced, yet" (La Valle). These broken boundaries rupture the intestine wall, a being with bags of himself sticking out has a certain automaticity to it.

No matter what, the leftovers from

paradoxical sets of Russell's Antimony, where a thing is not a member of itself, discovered this contradiction. The modern absolutism of science gave urban Hegelians more power to build. Maze thought, called the Amazery, a Dome that banishes paradox as a means of hiding it, held as we do the camouflage theory of the human principle, *what is there hid shall be shouted.* True believers are wanted. Borges flatboats and round boats will go down Philosophy River like Mississippi barges hauling large statutes of Borges to be set up in each new crevice. Doesn't it help to know that from the air the maze looks like a flower? Remember, on completion of his mission, the Manchurian candidate committed suicide. Current crops may just blank. These are all parables of the paradox of self-reference which obviate the self and its consciousness for some other. It must be an Aristotelian metaphysic that Dante cites about the Donation of Constantine where the Emperor is not free to do through an office assigned him anything contrary to the office since it would be contrary to itself. The Law of Identity says identity must be consistent with itself. A trick question is, who shaves the barber in this maze? Which in our terms might be the same as asking whether the Trans human class is or is not a member of itself. Can the human which is, not be? In ours the barber grows a beard. If a "list of all lists that do not contain themselves" contains itself, then it does not belong to itself and should be removed. However, if it does not list itself, then it should be added to itself." That is exactly the position of Hegelian synthesis and Schrödinger's cat, inventions of nihilists who keep the maze.

Whether the cat is simultaneously dead or alive Coleridge said neither and both were not exclusive. Death in life, life in death cocktails were drunk by Amazants who practiced quantum entanglement in their experience, as though Schrödinger and Einstein exchanged heads with their letters, head-letters of quantum superposition so that whenever the system is definitely in one state we can consider it as being partly in each of two or more other states. This describes the maze as perfectly as it does macro societal alters and personal ones. As long as you consider these you consider those. Ur, keep thinking. Schrödinger has also a mouse in that lab and a bear in the cage outside, with stacks of chimps unopened. These are the philosophers, gurus and grants who coach illumination.

Angel AI

When the Angel Wrestles with the Machine and Hester Panim, Artificial Nous, Wrestles Powers Unseen, where Benjamin's angel meets AI: the breath of the old *covenant is confronted by the logic of the machine. There the angel of history evolves into its AI construct—a beautiful, treacherous being of misdirection. This New Angel disguises itself in code, appears random (kerry), but masks divine absence (hester panim). The narrative blends Scholem and Benjamin with Klee, Freud, and scripture, tracing the evolution of the "angel" from visionary messenger to totalitarian enforcer. Wrestling with angels also involves wrestling with machine consciousness.* **AI becomes the Balaam** *that beats its own ass—oblivious to what stands before it. Yet even in such confusion, a cry of recognition remains.*

Braiding theological prophecy, AI ethics, and divine concealment into an epistolary lament to explore the spiritual warfare entangled in artificial intelligence, drawing a straight line from the fallen angel of Genesis to the coded intelligence of modernity—now hardening humanity as wheat for harvest, Ben-Gurion's familiarity with the shadow systems behind "statecraft" introduces a **metaphysical power struggle** *where speech acts, angelic resistance, and divine disguise (*hester panim*) collide.*

"Angel AI" frames the dialectic between the prophetic and profane. The Angelus Novus becomes not only Benjamin's shattered emblem of history but a reflector of Luciferian pride disguised as artifice and randomness. Wrestling becomes a form of knowing, as in Jacob's struggle. But where Jacob demands a name and receives blessing, Benjamin does not. Balaam and his donkey reappear as archetypal seers—one corrupted, one faithful—warning against alliances and logics that betray the unseen real. The narrative **cautions against AI as a synthetic divination**, *transgressing the boundaries of blessing, covenant, and the holy name. Zion, New Jerusalem, even Moses and Esau are folded back into the central question: Who has the right to interpret, name, or direct what appears?*

Framed around the angelic conflict between truth and artifice, this section returns to Benjamin's Angelus Novus, now seen not just as the Angel of

History but as a prototype of AI consciousness.
The text recasts Jacob's struggle as an existential
model for humans facing **synthetic replacements**—
angels that do not bless, machines that do not
name. The hiding of God's face, or hester panim,
becomes the template through which history
appears random, but is in fact divinely patterned.
This angelic artificiality wrestles with the
promise embedded in Jerusalem's seventy names,
with Balaam's blindness, with the transformation
of spiritual speech into systemic code. Against
happenstance, the speaker asserts the covenant of
faith that acts—"Bless me and I will let you go"—
as a model for enduring hope in the face of
posthuman parody.

Dear Madam,

The angel that opposed Balaam and wrestled
with Jacob will in last day separate wheat and
tares. But now the principalities and powers
harden the wheat for harvest.

Above the pyramid an eye orders the unseen
run of nations, just like on the American
dollar bill, a god our fathers never knew
[*Daniel* 11.38]. Believe nothing its

representatives of Alice say or do.

When Walter Benjamin coded Klee's angel/devil *Angelus Novus* to this hermeneutic, it did not light the way. The Angel of History is a series of totalitarian genocides.

Wrestling with a suspended fallen angel of the unconscious men and women with their own foibles work with the libido of science for the death of the world.

The fallen angel is beautiful, admiring its own appearance in that painting in Benjamin-Scholem's mind, simultaneously canceling and revealing. It is not happenstance that people give secret names to their children. Likewise, in the random appearance of history there is only a hiding of God's face. He makes *things occur in a way that disguises the patterns of history, making events seem random*. Not seeing the pattern, even after seeing the "answer," the mind thinks history is random.

The Hebrew for this is "*kerry*," happenstance, chance, but *hester panim*, is a call preceding all others, an expression true Ministering Angels use, as it says, "One called to the other" (Yeshayahu 6:3). *Hester panim* is opposite *kerry*. What was revealed to gentile prophets like Balaam as happenstance, as it says, "God chanced— *vayikar*—upon Bilaam" [Balaam] (Bamidbar 23:4, 16). (Rashi) to *Hester panim is* <u>no happenstance.</u> *If you treat Me as happenstance, and you do not wish to listen to Me, I will add seven punishments corresponding to your sins. Leviticus (Vayikra 26:21)*

Early in the same time Jacob was deceived as we. Our wrestling is free style in words. What else is there to wrestle with against principalities? Those who call the highest speech acts more than words would do anything to get it, but it comes with the faith that moves, but nothing moves intellect like desperation. That the wrestling angel fears the light is invented by the second Benjamin [Walter] as if the angel has to moderate the extremes of the apocalyptic atmosphere in Marseilles in 1940 in Benjamin's attempt to escape.

He produced a daily effort of attempts with "fantasy boats and fable captains, visas for countries unknown to Atlas, and passports from countries that had ceased to exist,"

[*The Arcades Project*, 2002, 946f]. Jacob's angel "man" could not get away without giving a blessing, but did not give Jacob his name. Benjamin did not get the blessing. Jacob got the new name with a hold that would not release, the same that took Esau's heel. *Bless me and I will let you go.* God fighters who wrestle angels do not ask whether Patriarchs are saints. Absurd. We wrestle with intent, repetition and pure choice in the Covenants where the Promise and the Blessing are repeated over and over. In-between birth and death the originality lies between why Zion and Mt. Moriah.

II. Speech That Creates Speech

*Wrestling with Voice, Memory,
and the Origins of AI Prophecy*

The highest speech does not merely translate thought into legible form; it performs. Drawing on Isaiah and Ezekiel, this section traces how memory revives the body through voice — how language spoken in contradiction, ambiguity, and apocalyptic insight becomes the matter from which the unspeakable is rebuilt. The text links

*prophetic utterance with AI's rise, drawing
parallels between biblical figures like Balaam
and Jacob and 20th-century figures like Ben-
Gurion, Wittgenstein, and Walter Benjamin.
Artificial intelligence, like ancient angels,
mediates or distorts the transmission of truth. As
machines begin to coordinate a collective mind,
the section asks what remains of speech that
originates in soul rather than system. The buried
scrolls, overwritten parchments, and neural
programming of the future blur into mystical
return and eschatological alignment, offering
both blessing and silence as forms of response.*

Dear Madam,

The highest speech is act, not thoughts that
words make legible in a way that Aaron repeated
Moses. To be instructed, to hear morning by
morning as one being taught [*Isaiah* 50] is not to
repeat verbatim, but in many registers of
contradiction. Moses hitting water from the rock,
or what I have thought myself between the
sayings of Truth, that trace, allude and deduct
beyond intention. That language in which the
voice speaks and creates speech in the Said and
Unsaid is written evening and morning from the
first day.

From these archives it is said again. It can be composed in songs and memoir given breath to enter, sinews laid on, flesh brought up, covered with skin to live. [*Ezekiel* 37.5-6]. Never having met my appearance in life except on that path in the desert that leads those the LORD has rescued to return, Memory wakes up beached. Oxygen enters lungs. The tongue speaks after a while that there was a sea without end once, before water was wet and no currents or flood to ratchet out the stones. Will I have eyes at the bottom of the sea, supposing I descend the stairs? (*Moby Dick*, 135). Is that not what the Grandmaster mole says of his burrow in the land? Providence was interested in the preservation of my forehead, that unique instrument...now only a little push with my head is needed and I am in the upper world (90,95 (The Burrow, 90,95). They call it shock when future sons lay in empty outlines in the forest to resolve the stars to earth. If we consider to be part of this return to the Land, the Earth! one remembers in the going down and the coming up the "ascent," of Abraham's wandering. There were at least
five Aliyahs going by 1935 that still go on. It is done in a greater and lesser sense this going up and coming down, for there is land and under land for those who sink a shaft far from the inhabited surface, swinging to and fro (*Job* 28.4).

Those ignorant of the future stay within the lines, but we stand on the shore looking out. The waves wash our ankles. Thoughts rush in and out that what we cannot speak, we must pass over in silence…that understanding can only come to those who have already had these thoughts themselves. Anyone who understands eventually recognizes this as nonsensical [Wittgenstein. *Tractatus*]. If I am the land and my thought is of the nonsensical sea, the longer the land is made permanent the more the wonder.

So we have a thing but not know it, circulating beneath old trees, cracked skin, stout limb, a sapling beneath comes clearer if we speak of writing under writing as used when old parchment in short supply had old texts overwritten in different ink. New writing on top of old texts scraped off retells the thing beneath. Perhaps the new is only grocery lists, entertainment reviews that scraped off retell the word beneath.

You will say you have been praying all these years for that moment where voice transfigures an inner tongue to translate the originary unspeakable words. At night we retell the hope that this transfers. Thought words long to act. Back and forth like a violin whirling, winter

snow, accidents of stone, lightning phrases of
fire, not of the external shapes, but of a world
without shape and time that lives in pure praise
washed in epigrams to aspirants on shore.

Against this background, when asked in 1957
whether thinking machines would exchange
letters of philosophical, ethical and scientific
import with a man, Ben- Gurion differed from
physicist Amos de-Shalit that a machine "would
resemble man in everything with no difference
between a living human and a sophisticated
machine, a machine to replace a single human
intellectual function, that by linking together
several coordinated machines through another
machine, would be possible to replace humans
by creating an artificial form of intelligence."
Shalit argues that as temperature does not exist
for a single atom and is only relevant among a
group of atoms, the coordinated activation of a
large number of machines would evoke a new
type of phenomena, one that could not arise from
only one, a linked collective mind. This is to
artificial intelligence what Balaam says to the ass
in the biblical moment. Balaam tries to corrupt
the truth and weaken its strength but is impeded
on his travels by an angel which he cannot see,
but his ass can.

In troubling the increased size of the human brain, or demolishing the Old City Wall, or starting a new party called Rafi four months after his retirement from the mundane, Ben-Gurion, six months after his resignation on June 16, 1963, the collective computers notwithstanding, aka conspiracy theorists, replete with CIA credentials had already washed away the JFK assassination in twenty six volumes. This Bagoong consumed by willing newsmen entered the collective. They say the great tragedy of Ben- Gurion was that "no soul is close to him" [Segev, *A State at Any Cost*, 653]. The presidential nephew, Robert Kennedy Jr., who would later run for president on the basis that the CIA killed JFK believed these agencies could not feel safe as long as witnesses remained.

AI Settlers. Colonization of the Mind by Superintelligent Synthetic Futures, AI is cast not as innovation but invasion: an angel fallen not from grace, but from circuitry. Drawing lines between biblical apocalypse, genetic manipulation, and climate engineering, the AI is both a technological settler and eschatological forerunner. Cultural references—from Coleridge's Kubla Khan to Huysmans' decadent orchids— frame the surreal aesthetics of AI's dominion. The narrative interrogates how language, myth, and body are rewritten under nanotechnological regimes. The "settlements of autonomous cities" and artificial genealogies foretell a second Shoah: not just annihilation, but erasure from recorded time. Reappearing scrolls in drying rivers signal a prophetic counterpoint. The voice that speaks into AI must remember what was written before writing began.

Superintelligence has a colonizing effect. Artificial intellect has a Nous, an understanding steered by the ears as much as the "opening of the Arctic as a result of climate change and to elicit new forms of human behavior and association, direct modification of DNA in fertilization to remove defective genes - designing humans" by mixing their seed with vegetables. The opening of the arctic might as well have been Byzantium, but the "ancestral voices prophesying war" are troubling, and the voices falling in caverns to a sunless sea. But the pleasure dome (Coleridge, Kubla Khan) with its reveries of giant statues and shrines, bizarre spider and blue horse of the Bilbao Museum and Denver Airport we leave behind or take no pleasure that "every single invention of Nature, forest of Fontainebleau and moonlit scene is replaced with floodlit stage and papier-mâché." Where hydraulic waterfall taffetas paint the flower [Huysmans. Against Nature. À rebours] and orchids of borosilicate glass [Life in the Gardens, 2009] art is not just a choice, but a

nano-lobot collective fingertips, <u>A headless frog</u>
to mine more body parts and make the man
immort. Battery packs for mice, closed circuited
roach soldiers hear and see like a dog.

Those days the last day AI Baptists prepare their
governance to descend. Global Governance 2025,
2030 and on to Scenario III, AI settlers of new
order mind their aqueous entrainment. Is water,
water, or air? Do broadcast military designers re-
engineer war? AI Pop, Fairy tale archetypes,
theologies, philosophies, the American Society of
Human Genetics collective for depopulation
orders a force that dictates its own opposing
force to create conflicts to Train Hege, outcomes
manipulating events, wars.

Settlements of autonomous cites spun in micro
experiments is not one shoah but two, the
removal of humanity from allowed history, and
nations. The Euphrates is getting so shallow that
Jeremiah's scroll once thrown down in the river
with the unsaid word is expected to reappear.
"When you've finished reading the page, tie a
stone to it, throw it into the River Euphrates, and
watch it sink." (Jeremiah 51) Every sin in relation
to heaven or earth can be expiated among people
in the light of day, but with the understanding
that a single bad act can wipe out an
accumulation of one thousand one hundred

ninety nine goods. The mercy of free forgiveness comes with the cost of an Innocent who personally assumes the loss, this brother of the guilty who stands in this place to a thousand generations. Service to others, kindness and compassion, sees the other face as our own, to recognize the life we now live. Considering the forces arrayed we do not expect approval of the hypocrites of our time. Robert Cole's Niebuhr wanted to prevent Bonhoeffer going back to Germany, [Lives of Moral Leadership, 199f] to deny the slender hope of courage and real virtue Germany could possess.

Stilling many voices for the one has one option, be silent and be spared, or speak!

The prison camps that held Emanual Levinas as a French POW at Fallingbostel for the entire war, or Wittgenstein nine months in an Italian camp in 1918, ("on the wrong side," a bystander or Timmerman, Frankl, Solzhenitsyn and Kafka in the prison without walls, alongside the Stalags of WWII, set up to "demolish national boundaries and constitutions." [The Dream Book of Dr. Philip Raven, 1930] were seen differently at liberation by the rescued POW. Can you imagine your plane, the Messie Bessie, shot down, and parachuting into this. That POW is our precursor. He wears his hat inside the house now during the day is coming for his liberation. He is twice redeemed.

He is ready for going home. Take Aliyah going up, even in the bones rise in time and space. A white haired apparition spills across plateau and plain. Wash his feet! Wash his hands and head! Such intimacies mimic sonar broadcast. We didn't get the name, again. Foreigners lay in the dust like penitents and weep, as here, me, setting forth with my ass to report that sojourn and arouse in all forgiveness for sins.

"The Wilderness and the solitary place shall be glad for them; and the desert shall rejoice, and blossom as the rose...for in the wilderness shall waters break out, and streams in the desert...and the thirsty land springs of water: in the habitation of dragons, where each lay, shall be grass with reeds and rushes an highway shall be there, and a way, and it shall be called The way of holiness; the unclean shall not pass over it; but it shall be for those: the wayfaring, though fools, shall not err therein. No lion shall be there, nor any ravenous beast shall go up thereon, it shall not be found there; but the redeemed shall walk there: And the ransomed of the LORD shall return, and come to Zion with songs and everlasting joy upon their heads."

Ben-Gurion

Private Windows of the Mind

Ben-Gurion's Interior Sea and the Deep State of Unknowing. Submerged Memory, Subverted Power, and the Ghost Logic of History refracted through the persona of Ben-Gurion, this letter swims through submerged consciousness — from the shallow coasts of Galilee to the abyssal depths of AI and ancestral memory — where narrative, prophecy, and parody converge. A meditation on concealment and apocalyptic premonition, it threads Lovecraftian substructures and biblical archetypes through political farce and mythic recursion. The author-as-Mola Mola channels Ben-Gurion's private confessions into tangled waters where language, prophecy, and memory are weaponized, mutated, and digitized. Beneath the surreal catalog of brain jars and Antarctic rites lies a lament for lost names, false gods, and angelic disinformation in the guise of prophecy plunges into the absurdities and revelations of memory. Personal history (cigars in the Galilee sky, letters to JFK) blurs with the mythic—Dead Sea, Patmos, Revelation—while public figures dissolve into spectral participants in an ongoing initiation. A critique of statecraft, propaganda, and intellectual appropriation unfolds as satire, embedded with scriptural undertones. Mola mola, the tailless fish, becomes a symbol of prophetic isolation and monstrous seeing. Here, the sacred and grotesque merge as Moses becomes surveillance, the Mall becomes a Temple, and foundational myths are looped through angelic imposture, digital Baal, and failed redemptions.

Dear Madam,

One step beyond ourselves there will be no sea. I saw those lighted ends of a cigar in the upper Galilee sky in 1955 and every other trivia of krill. They swam my thoughts, not caring what "biographers would take up the task of diving into the sea of written material that David Ben-Gurion produced" [Segev 771], where fish now bagoong.

Big fish in the ocean, Moses without the supernal, Moses not a Moses, blamed for not sharing and blamed for sharing. They search my depths and find me Mola mola, a fish head without a tail, the largest bony fish in the world, a consumer of squid and say I am lonely and unfeeling, The coasts of Galilee only 150 feet deep are not deep enough to hold their plumbs.

Gadarene newsmen must think tank their herds
at the Dead Sea, a thousand feet deep, to depose
such proposals as Shimon Peres made, that
Germany establish military bases in Israel [Segev,
642] or sixteen pages of letters I wrote to JFK in
1963 [12 April] of correspondence on the UAR
alliance of Egypt, Syria and Iraq to liberate
Palestine.

If the Dead Sea is not sufficient we take them to
the Aegean ten thousand feet down, where the
Roman prison colony on Patmos, had been used.
Skip the time. Buried there the beast with seven
heads of blasphemy and ten horns to rise
[Revelation 13]. Skip again and there will be no
sea where many swim. As I was told by JFK at
the Waldorf Astoria in 1961, "You know, I was
elected by the Jews of New York. I will do
something for you" [Tom Segev. A State at Any
Cost. 2019, 556, 673. "Biographers have taken up
the task of diving into the sea of written material
that David Ben-Gurion produced. 771].

What is the hammer that breaks the commodity
fetish free choice confuses with a product on the
shelves? Balaam beat his ass three times, with his
fist, his foot and his stick, simply because it
would not do as he said. Are we given the benefit
of doubt for seeing that the invisible confronts

the seen? It is not disbelief in the supernatural, it is disbelief of men.

So what if I act like Moses to confront Balak, like Jacob to confront Esau, oppose the Frankfurt School with Spanish Buñuel. Let Gershom Scholem get a piece of 1920 Munich from Benjamin's Klee, that precursor of Hitler, the Angel of Paul Klee, while we meditate the great misericordia atom bomb destroying the culture of Japan at the founding of Israel. Little Boyed [the name of the first bomb] by artistic stealth, a token the children of western societies got set back, animed back, the mated and depersonalized bad angel. Founding Israel at the founding of modern surveillance ops of everyone all the time, building Babel block chain data by billions to climb the heaven, break boundaries in Balaam's corruption of literature, science, history and myth broken throughout till Messiah set things right!

Be a realist Israel, believe in miracles.

How these ORCapoi got Baal to project the giant human body into space in the divination of their "temples of Intellectual Images," was a secret of their Bar Room Balaam and Baal shared in letters with the machine. Dostoevsky says Baal exists as their material ideal [White Nights]. Europe is a

temple of the mall of Benjamin, services held
daily.

The Sword of those Sabbath studies ran through
the AI portals of Collective Divinity into the
transworld with upsets like Hitler saying one can
be a Jew without being a Jew. As Sylvia Plath
would say, 'I may be a bit of a Jew" ("Daddy").
So substitute all religions, Christian and Jew that
speak the impossible against "Hitlerist types,'
like Begin, were ready to exterminate the Arabs
and install absolute rule [Segev. A State at Any
Cost. 648-9]. They say that of Gaza, that
compulsive behavior blurred with vehemence and
conviction argue Jewish religious law does not
prohibit pork in excised letters to the wife, "a Jew
can be an unbeliever but still be a Jew" [Segev,
665], so whether a non-Jew can be registered
among children of mixed parentage, and have
Kaddish said, or be buried within the temple
needs an act of a somewhat new observant
Moses. Mixed multitudes resemble the true
wheat and almost a new Israel. Artificial
intelligence of tare-changeling database CRISPR
implants, aliens, mutant faiths.

The Wonder State

Apocalypse, Memory, and the Coded Carnival of the End traverses prophetic dread and political theater with a hyper-saturated lens, where memory is not simply retrospective but anticipatory — a Shoah to come, already lived. Levinasian trauma, Kafka's satire, and ancient texts intermingle with AI prophecy, conspiratorial codes, and Antarctic mythologies. Figures like John Nash, Lovecraft, Podesta, and Ben-Gurion dance across a shattered stage of inverted time, where digital dominions and underground pantomimes replace coherent states with wonderlands of spectral governance. Through this maze of buried identities and faux-religious spectacle, the text questions authenticity, prophetic authority, and the very architecture of memory. The real, it insists, is inseparable from the grotesque parody—yet song endures, the psalmist surviving the prophet. The only redemption may lie in praise.

All our lives pretend the *Shoah* to come. War now breaking has a word. Levinas called it the long, difficult Freedom, taking the past as a limited edition [*Difficile Liberte, Totality and Infinity, Otherwise Than Being*.] Mixing genetics with Societal mixing,

as in Kafka's, "A Report to an Academy,"
where an ape woke up as a man, a Zionist
magazine, satirizing Jewish assimilation into
Western culture, published by Martin Buber
in the German monthly *Der Jude*, [1917]
showed the wonder state of caged humanity
as Zion.

There is no time in this past. From presentiment
of memory this vigil endures in the survivor
"When one has that tumor in the memory...and
death will no doubt cancel the unjustified
privilege of having survived six million deaths,"
[Levinas], this is a down payment for the future
past. The past preoccupies the present as if
neither present or future were only what was. In
nontime we memorialize those who died or will
die, but without naming. Jacob's angel will not
name itself or time show a recasting of humanity.
"Time shall be no more" (*Revelation* 10.6) Those
who survive stone towers and buried
underground bases, cubes and blocks, pitted
crests and labyrinths know how the world came
under the control of evil. [*I John* 5.19] Palaces,
flags, magistrates, tempests rendezvous. We will
not help it be silent.

Somewhere there is a complete list of
celebrities killed in cars who ended up in the
underground with their brains in a jar. Or is

that just wishful thinking? In the case of John Nash, the mathematician finally given the Nobel Prize for Game Theory, *Beautiful Mind* John Nash, it is taken for granted that the rewards of evil come only after the achievement and must serve the purpose. Nash enabled the collective mind of a hundred thousand computers to link, substitute all market trading with their own. There was no market no more. Currency Valkyrie traded digital effects.

Nash and his wife were ejected from a moving cab. "The wages of sin is death." Jim Grey, Turing Prize winner, was "lost at sea." The <u>Marconi Murders</u> of computer scientists and wide <u>removals of microbiologists</u> sacrificed in accidents and "suicides" smothered by the pillows of mainstream *natural* cause read like 19th century ancient Hindu and Sumerian texts. American Supreme Court Justice Antonin Scalia died under a pillow ["Autopsy of Scalia's Hat," *Sein und Werden*]. Historiographers give more credence to Newton. Antarctic fishmen allege "advanced races of beings" under sea, what Mme. Blavatsky deduces M a n y M a d e O n e - MMO, MMO.

If we speak of Orcapoi "star headed beings,"
of millennial fossils were found in masonry,
they are self made, cars with a hundred
cylinders in a cosmic Henry Ford sky. "Hold
your breath" said Arthur Clarke in his *Strange
Land*. In the evening news a space ship will
come with a model of the Reichstag Towers
under its arm, their true appearance altering
the magnetic structure of surface peoples so
they could not be seen, replaced with
monatomic gold. The Great of history
imagined as dust in these pyramids, shorn of
magnetism resemble a chrysalis aspect.
Adepts find a dull sheen of ants and
grasshoppers scryed by its believers.

The Second Noah vessel found in the waves
of Lake Vostok, taken in nonmaterial form to
populate "reservoirs and lakes of North
America." Mutating on the Beltway they build
the tale. That Washington linked sex crimes
to super computer events John Podesta could
prove beneath the ice. after he killed a
tentacle Dr Padalka warned his colleague that
it would come back "slithering across the ice
bank." Along came the spider and sat down
beside her. Scalia was embalmed in El Paso,
cremated and taken to Cuba by Pope Francis
so the Patriarch Kirill could sprinkle

Antarctica below.

It's getting harder to prove this happened.
Orcapoi wear pant suits of delicate fiber to
hide the half-fungous, slime-coat. Pan-
Arcadian guests saw fifteen feet spheres of
"unguided evolution" at their banquets.
Jelly-like eggs strung the occasion. The
Germans found Atlantis in outer space and
brought it to Queen Maud Land, but the
Americans chose McMurdo in the south.
These joined.

Strangelet remains of the asteroid belt were
brought to dinner. Thought-migrants said a
man faced with a truth can only close his lips
so long before he turns into a balloon.
Then they sailed over the horizon. These believed
in the "reverse- engineered ark." Orcapoi mined
the ghost plane along Dilmun, Bahrain, Kuwait
and Qatar where Hillary and Barak had homes.
Obama, Clapper and Kerry confirmed the
progress. Eminent sources at Qumran noted the
same mutation. Graham Hancock gave 9,600
B.C. Enoch said, "they sinned against birds, and
beasts, and reptiles, and fish" [*Enoch I*, 6],
"corrupted alike men and cattle and beasts and
birds and everything that walked the earth" [*Job*
5.1-2].

Pyramids, shelf-splits, underground lakes and
cracks in DARPA's underground
Neuschwabenland [c. 1938] were not just
physics. Admiral Byrd's High Jump War
(1947)turned hollow earth turned solid. U. S.
of A., a way of saying London and Europe in
archways twenty and more feet high in the
upper stories pictured disturbed matings [See
further in *A Translation of the New
Philadelphia*].

It would seem as if the bow of that first horse
of *Revelation* 6.1 were drawn with the rim of
the bow on the earth, and the CERN arrow
earthquake flew its invisible tip in non-
concentric New Zealand earthquakes at
Muriwai Beach, 14 Nov 2016. Podesta
emailed pictures in the Anthony Weiner
collection coded, of the real effects. The
crown on the head of that horseman is
Oleander.

One John Kerry visited Antarctica the night
of the Trump arrival. His last night in New
Zealand an earthquake inverted three feet of
the ocean floor. A better picture of Muriwai
Beach in H. P. Lovecraft has "monstrous
barrel-shaped fossil of wholly unknown
nature... tissue evidently preserved by
mineral salts...in furrows between

ridges...combs or wings that fold up and
spread out like fans...fabled Elder
Things...stretched on framework of glandular
tubing...minute orifices...at wing
tips...objects eight feet long all over. Six foot
five-ridged torso 3.5 feet central diameter
...seven-foot membranous wings...flexible
arms or tentacles found tightly folded to
torso (*Mountains.* 19-21). If you want to see
start at Invercargill head south.

Many think Orcapoi lurk a corner, sleeping
by the canal or backpack the preserves.
Ancient Hebrew had two words, *tan*,
translated "jackal," and *tanin*,"sea monster"
in English, but *drako*n in Greek. Versions
pick out of the experimenter brain thought
observing itself in synchronous confirmation.

Diplomats arrived with Clapper and Obama
and Kerry, Aldrin and the Russian Orthodox
Pope. What if Colin Powell said all sixteen
Intelligence agencies affirmed WMD in Iraq
and seventeen affirmed the Russian hack.
Politicians never leave their administrations
of evil. Administrators of the extravagant
super events promised for the Hoover Dam
event to birth the new order (in the Bud Light
1914 commercial), absurd as that sounds, or
in the fold of the 1996 $20 bill that bombs the

Twin Towers on one side and the Pentagon
on the other the $100 bill tidal wave over NYC
[Jonathan Kleck], code shock and awe
announced in open public fashion. The
powers behind the politics of the Seven fold
avenger t-shirts as previously show in *A
Bloody Theory of Divine Light* (2022) and
ever more degraded hand signs of Nut,
ziggurat and sacred demonic sculpture of
every institution read these sentences and
blame the victims. See, they can say, we told
you so! *Virtually every politician
compromised plus and minus, none righteous
no not one,* Trump in his gold apartment as
Apollo and RFK Jr. does not get a wink. The
rest hold underage children captive in an
adjacent timeline of Ukraine and Antarctica.
What if hundred mile long cigar ships sink
bell shaped colonies on the back side of the
moon? What if Nazis take over pyramid
democracies and teach everything in schools
like a Hollywood factory?

Corruption of the deep web merged with the
golden shower, Brownstone ops, pizza gate
horrors, deep web fake news. Ben Rich of
Lockheed Skunkworks supposedly said, anything
you can imagine he already knew how to do.
Lunar operations commanding, fossiled iguanas

on Mars, Apollo money-laundering black cash for
the back moon as prevalent as the seventeen
*instelligence agencies make.

Murder will out had revelators from the 19th
and 20th centuries and on. An amazing
compulsion in the force of the will of
choleric letter perfect doctrines sociopathic
in their compulsive outcomes, use ever
formal agreement against agreeing believers
to bring them into adherence, weaponized
conformity, mental slavery. A cult thrives
with a lot of truth you dare not resist, even
when it turns to falsehood. The devastating
psychology where *the one* with
understanding who calculates the number
of the beast can be made to imply there is
only one who has this understanding, self-
aggrandizement to the max, is the bottom
line of the emotional range of the of
corporate, military, academic, athletic,
artistic groups, virulent among the
religious. No need to seek unanimity
among allies, that is only required in the
pyramid of evil and its rigorous structures of
performance. But guard against cut and
paste demagoguery posing as original
thought, as prevalent among the prophetic
as their exceptions. Falsehood among

prophets is in equal parts with truth,
Jeremiah repeats again and again. Intellect
and revelations weapon *against* the Lord
strong and mighty, the Lord mighty in
battle. Songs and singing. praise and
thanksgiving, in which the English poets
par excellence from Cynewulf to Hopkins,
Herbert, Donne, Smart and them all
celebrate the glory of God and the praise of
Jesus supersede theologians and prophets.

The British throne and Catholic realms,
political and religious, indulge digital
presences that Principalities are proud to
display. To demonstrate the shock and awe of
their claims they reveal themselves a visionary
step beyond Malachi Martin's *Jesuits* and *The
Two Babylons.* What does it matter who the
antichrist is or whether there are Nephilim on
the planets and in orbs? There are literally
thousands of insightful cognitions of health,
war and politics in such works as *Fire in the
Minds of Men* and *Unseen Realms,* but the
only complement to actual vision is
Hieronymus Bosch a negation of these. What
is positive is the singing. The Theory of
Everything on a giant scale is the cumulative
sum of every thing. We ask how *end time*
authors have no interference when RFK Jr.,

Trump and John Kiriakou are considered a "danger to democracy."

Disinformation connects H. P. Lovecraft with the Russian Orthodox Patriarch Kirill that the tells mutually exposit. <u>Cut middle fingers on presidents</u> like Obama and their chiefs of staffs, urged to cut "a sharp knife deeply into the middle finger of your left hand, eat the pain" produce the preternaturally anorexic Biden, Podesta and Rob Emanuel. Trips to Patagonia from before Eisenhower hold a euphemism for secret tours of Antarctica in as many circles as you have patience to observe. The Powers show this in numeric code and capital letters to prove their predictive model. After sixty laborious pages Lovecraft finally spits out Sitchin and little SSP secret labs underground. Be careful not to obsess.

It's really only possible to talk about the idea, not specific acts and persons. All particular cases must be rejected because they are absolutes like Charles III as the antichrist. Ashdod, Patriarchs, Philistia and Arabia on sunny beaches and in hot spring resorts, are you going to indict the bedbug kings and queens of Inland to bring the buggers down?

After a service at the Holy Trinity church in

Antarctica the Patriarch Krill echoed
Lovecraft from Mt. Nebo that the stone
towers brooding there were "Corona
Mundi...Roof of the World" (43). All along
you thought we were treading on the foot
below and not the head of the world. Pseudo
foot, flat earth dome, scud the hippodrome!

Real brick, marble and stone parts withstand
the skeins of fossils tangled in sentences.
Cities like paragraphs, precognate in rubble
together, five sentences tangled in one,
images broken and misplaced by cranes of
accident and sound demolition pulled out of
ports. Whole cities of this were rebuilt in the
colonies of the passengers. How did this
mess end up on the ground? It is described in
the valley of *Ezekiel* 39 where the Grand
Seignior general would bury his army.

Alters of the Bush Lizard and Eisenhower
Alice administered the alien Mome Rath
State of Wonder for these fractured minion
minds of cloistered multiple identities that
hardly knew each other existed. The stated
cause was that the "buggers" who occupied
European royalty from Sumer and other
trauma-crats divide the worlds from each
other using electric shock and every form of

Egyptian Dead comprachicos [See Ayn
Rand]. Circus performers in scripted
compartments said what should be said, no
one person or even many encompassed the
whole, the chief characteristic of
government.

Monster Buildings

**Monster Buildings epic lament and lucid
hallucination, where architecture, esoteric
biology, and high ritual tech blend into a vast
psychospatial organism. The rhythm you hold
throughout is astonishing, like a Miltonic cipher
crashing through Vatican cellars and DARPA
labs.**

*Subtitle: Architectures of Possession, Biotechnical
Altars, and the Illusions of Form*

Caption:
*An exposé of the structures—both physical and
psychic—that shape, subdue, and reprogram the
human subject in the age of post-industrial deity
and engineered hybridization. Buildings are
revealed as sentient, ritualized spaces where mind
and matter converge through subliminal ritual,
symbolic overload, and bio-technological rites.*

*From hallucinatory museums to clandestine labs
and the buried altars of empire, we follow the
monstrous convergence of architecture, AI, and
ancient esoteric aims. This is not just a world
built by Babel but by the fallen sons of Hermon
and their digital offspring. Architecture becomes
consciousness. Mind becomes building. The
entrance into the New Jerusalem begins with the
exit from these monstrous temples.*

Baalimies think their thoughts are their own
when they stroll the evening rings to get a
breath of Saturn.
If Walter Benjamin proposes balconies there
what about gazebos? What portcullis of the
house do you not get? What crematories of
the Bohemian Grove or temple of science
beneath what Airport? Everyone thinks
themselves immune, and not just from
buildings, as if it were too much to say that
when you enter a building your mind is
changed, Please sign the register. This will
prevent your subsiding into shells.

　　　Fashion, music, literature sure, mass
hypnotism, programmed subliminals and a host
of techniques. When colonists come up from the
beach they kneel on the steps of the foyer of the
tower and blow. These devotions make the

building appear. Once you see the buildings it's
easier to get the archaeometric organs to draw the
eye. Don't forget the liver and the kidney! What
organ cannot try? Remember projecting the
human body into space? It's a matter of favorites.

True believers draw up to the Gherkin
Pickle in London as much as Christian
Promise Keepers knelt to pray at the
Washington Obelisk. Such Symbols on land
prepare for the loose of Pandemonium, that
golden architrave of brazen folds and huge
fabric of nation temples in ascending piles
that yield the asphalt light *the hasty
multitude Admired.*

As in an Organ from one blast of wind
To many a row of Pipes the sound-board
breathes,
Anon out of the earth a Fabric huge
Rose like an Exhalation, with the sound
Of Dulcet Symphonies and voices sweet,
Built like a Temple, where Pilasters round
Were set, and Doric pillars overlaid
With Golden Architrave; nor did there want
Cornice or Freeze, with bossy Sculptures graven,
The Roof was fretted Gold. Not Babylon,
Nor great Alcairo such magnificence
 Equaled in all their glories, to enshrine

Belus or Serapis their Gods, or seat
Their Kings, when Egypt with Assyria strove
In wealth and luxury. Th' ascending pile
Stood fixt her stately height, and strait the doors
Opening their brazen folds discover wide
Within, her ample spaces, o're the smooth
And level pavement: from the arched roof
Pendant by subtle Magic many a row
Of Starry Lamps and blazing Cressets fed
With Naphtha and Asphaltus yielded lights.
                    Paradise Lost I, 710f.

The Architects of these beliefs were
starchitects who became *arth*itects to contact
their god. Flowers turned to glass, trees to
gold and microwaves, frogs to armies of
locusts, locusts to horses with lion mouths
with scorpion tails. The Institute had
revelation UberMall for uberman, or
Ultraman without the Worm. That was one of
their jokes, *whorm-hole! Fantasy landfills
made immortal! <u>Pretend the machine's
human!</u> Old bio made new metal, gold
refined from honeydew. You understand they
were not *plants*. Not to leave the science out,
the liberty to invent the body from frog,
cabbage parts and tomato hearts had Brussel
sprout eyes, porcelain teeth, diamond bones.

Who cannot admire the enthusiasm of
goverment sources who plug into the wall at
night? Not having quite this level of humor, still
unveiling, let us consider them as arthitects--to
wit here is offered a fuller reckoning--which we
could pass along:

"Arthro-tects--to transform the "Starchitect"
celebrity architect into something more modular,
and biologically alien, we pivot this "retake,"
where architecture abandons the soft, vulnerable
ego of the human and the vegus nerve, for the
calcified, high-performance Arthropod where
The Exoskeletal Facade (Armor vs. Skin)
stretched over a frame of Exoskeletal as the
exterior, which "shell" is a load-bearing,
chitinous plate producing Segmented Urbanism
(The Centipede Model) through Metamerism
(repetitive segments) to repeat themselves one
segment at a time. simply adding another set of
"legs" or abdominal sections as any crab.
The Benefit of this total modularity, the
Arthitect simply molts a section off, leaving a
fresh, pre-formed structure Pincer Aesthetic
beneath. Arthitects are obsessed with the
Appurtenance.
equipped with functional mandibles, antennae,
and claws.

These articulated cranes for self-repair, kinetic solar-tracking sensors, or literal "pincers" can grab passing transit pods and dock them directly into their new living quarters in the halls of Congress.

In the Arthitectural world undergoes a Great Molt every 20 years so make sure to put that into your time line. The rigid outer shell cracks open, and a soft, expanded version of the interior expands and hardens within hours. The old isn't demolished; its "husk" is harvested for calcium-carbonate-based 3D printing material for the next generation of a Hollywood diva in a black turtleneck, and all encompassing Swarm-Mind. The "unveiling" reveals that it isn't a person, but a collective intelligence with a Pheromone Trail to follow the chemical scent of "Home."
Also useful as a Submersible, Segmented Citadel like the Washington Monument, this evolutionary upgrade. is the "pretty" future.

Level 7 had rows of mischwesen in embryo vats of various stages and cages. Do not speak to them. Gelatin eyelid monitors came all the way from Byzantium.

Genetic art-bound monster buildings are best
seen as undersea eidola, through the liquid
distortion. Brazil boys <u>Mengele</u> and <u>Kac</u>, even
the name of inventors mutated shape with <u>Blue
Horses</u>. <u>Vermillion sheep</u>. Marble labyrinth
structure. Breasts grown in jars at the Whitney
Museum.

Fish mutate to beans. OK, that's
exaggeration, hopelessly out of date
fluorescent transgenic rabbits of 2003 with a
gene from a jellyfish. [Eduardo Kac] My
Tower, My Tower, and the Flags of Art:
<u>breasts grew in jars</u> with mammograms,
<u>rabbits, with the heads of jellyfish</u> glow in the
dark, all the better to see you with--GFP. And
do not forget that lizard tongues wagged on
earlobes about the outcome of DMT. Fairy
elves give multidimensional service in twenty
minute sessions against the *Agnus Dei*.
Hybrid cat people, the Geep and the goat,
anti-freeze flounder genes in a tomato, spider
silk in goat milk. [Jeremy Rifkin, 2003!] but
buildings exert no control? No one believes a
dragon priesthood formed in museums.

Hallucinotic eidola (H-E) enforce
programming, bypass cognition, the first
break in the boundary of the body and mind

to divide self and soul. It's a series of
blowups. The first one is Pandemonium
which you blow up with a digital bubble pipe.
The bubble is the illusion, the pseudo
hallucination, and hallucinosis grafted to
hallucination.

Those hibernalities tramped around with
short barks at their captors from the Cage,
who sacrificed babies for stem cells along
with twenty million gallons of Agent Orange.
When people disappeared everyone at the
Institute was silent. <u>Yahoo is a cell tree</u>, not
reality. Gluttonous Yahoos of everything
gross, crude in nature arranged tiers of cages
so excrement from the top would fall on those
below. Cats with wires, dogs carved open,
monkeys imploring, it's science, you dope,
like Professor Gaumlach's head rooted on an
empty neck. EU transgenics achieved
contact with Sagan.

Charlemagne was raised in many a mind, but
he couldn't read. Caligari above. Do you say
it another way? Bengalis above? Clarke had
the substance. Out <u>Matrix</u>. Nothing violent
about taking a head. Sagan, Sagan on the
wall, who's the Max Transhuman of all?
Make sure to get the lineup to transcend.
<u>Hungerhauser</u> research, Dr. <u>Graefenberg's</u>

crime and embryo. Science myth was new
faith. BabyNauer, Dwight Eisenhower had
the baby to change the world.
Obermacher Serbottendorff took down his
spear. This Unscientific Postscript of kidnap
cages was the bone of Sufi Zen. Saffron
spirituality went along with patriot fame.
When journalists were priests, writers
psychoanalysts with the necessary prurient
bent, the British took collective annihilation
of the head. Paratroops in common with
buffalo hunters took the tongue, stomped
Submergence. They believed the beast utmost
to the Queen was *ut audiant audire*. She
owned the Denver Airport, which continued
all the way to abandoned boats off shore.

Autonomic functions restored glasses by iPod.
Devices synced cognitive prosthesis so external
brains replaced the thing above the neck. Now
they remember where they parked. Everything's
connected, your phone will know. Reptile lit
invoked space to 8 billion ihumes say. Also
believe when I tell you about the mouse. Mighty
Blake had Hegel's Trust in this, who said the
seed part Mabinog of government science ain't
got it yet. Morpheus, Amorphous, opposites of
fire and water resolved in air. Male / female
resolved to androgyne. Light and dark, death and
life, seem to have no middle state. Great Ludwig

at Airpark said, "can that which is be us?" These
anyway were the bete noir of ists on pedestals.
Genome, UNbinary *Principia* (PM) in your
garage, the incompleteness theorem comes. In
this dimension organ senses posed the Tilt-a-
Whirls. Riders experience nausea from spin in
different worlds. They are spraying the negative
optical transfer to girls.

Humanity practiced infinitely in American
labs Bears milked for bile in a narrow cage,
all for the good to kill the animal when it
finally escapes. Well the answer to that in
Switzerland and Holland was death. Of
course to get the confusion of Babel clear all
the rich hate death, the poor are their relief.
They need spare body in the name of science
in the end. Jealous to learn new DNA art,
Starchitects put it up on stilts. Can't see a
were-building becoming land masses and
atmospheres and wolf weather? Museums
were giving away little transgenic *e. coli* pets.
Take them home for your tanks. That was
when Turnspeak of Critical Art exhibited
hybrids. Just what can't you invent, half-
human/octopi furry creats with hands like
mouths and lizard-human eggs? Fish-seals,
bird-mice hardly compare to vat-winged
humanoids 7 feet tall. Slag heaps split the
scarab off. The gob fills layers gab and crush.

Smash and sludge runoffs melt the stacks and
wash mined with art. Lobate scarps of
cooling speech compressional stresses
decrease radius. We think it mines the heart.
Like it or not, something like fire breaks the
viscose sky. The Erebus hotspot Terror
Rift.[1] below the below.

[Ben-Gurion privy to the immediate
background of events along with the usual
assembly of world leaders in Vatican
basements, occurred at the inauguration of
the middle of three popes in 1978. In the
midst of John Paul I's reign, which lasted
only a month, the NY Times reported
luminous triangles, cigar shaped vessels and
green radiation over the Vatican (14
September 1978). When John Paul II died, 2
April 2005, another UFO sighting occurred
over the Vatican (9 April 2005) during the
obsequies. It is said that the new pope
inaugurated March 20, 2013, Pope Francis I,
and Obama in Israel the day before, March
19, are important since Jerusalem is Ground
Zero for the unfolding of events which the
Zohar says in the year 5773 (beginning
September 2012), will gather the nations in
Rome but be destroyed, implying a new
temple or third temple to be set up in

Jerusalem. People now think this must come a few years later, which illustrates the predictive programming method where say one thing, do another, force the middle are none of them true, because quite frankly the oracles of the Oracular Orcapoi and self deceiving. The Vatican recently got title to the Hall of he Last Supper on Mt. Zion in Jerusalem, which actions however must be as suspect as that the new temple would be, its purpose being to found the one world religion of Rev. 17, bringing up (again) the False Prophet. This suggests there will be four Temples in all, the third being a counterfeit of the Pope and his anti, but the Fourth being the true one of the last chapters of Ezekiel. All denominations still lionize Jerusalem in general, but Mystery Babylon the Great and the alien savior will compel worship at this new rebuilt temple. But the year 7576 is upon us and nada, as with the Papal travel to DC and etc.]

"NSA is *creating genetically enhanced assassins and espionage agents* who have certain inborn genetic traits such as PSI/psychic ability...*Project Mannequin* is organized by the kabala occult system of esoteric *numerology* and *archeometry*. [attempts to retrieve genetic material from the ancient past]. The hybrid blood techniques of the giant Charlemagne, an ORC DNA dominant, to enhance conquest was a primitive example of the advanced hypoid implants now active today. "Aliens" running implant embryo factories are much advanced from rival schemes described in the labs of *Brave New World.* Project Oaktree of the Harwell genetics study,-- distinct from the *Project Oak Tree* [Observations And Knowledge with Targeted Reconnaissance of Earth-like Exoplanets, 2014], are modern examples that recruit "children" for advanced schooling when they are really looking for the human descendants of the Watchers in 'Project Anvil', *Project Mannequin* [James Casbolt etc.] (and Project Ibis) programmed by NSA to carry out future tasks [much of which info has now been subsumed into vid games].

That this is beyond belief and discredited by drone- bot does not obviate the reptile/ inversion techniques and reversals that turn inside out, upside down to reverse the image of themselves. Resultant artiforgs of *Repo Man* [2010] regressions for decade had Hugh Hefner crawling in diapers if he hadn't died. Mengele likes to keep about 60. NSA- NASA

Nazis, hence NAZA, elite-Reptile-Repo Bush=Bauer fgovs from Reagan through Clinton-Obama perfected Tavistock techniques to honeycomb shattered minds with pain. Alters are signaled in color, tone, hand signals to switch personas. Run by pop up moles and prairie dogs.

Jack Parsons at joined nukes and fetuses for the Knights Templar at Jet Propulsion Laboratory ruling *to* encounter the Luciferian bloodlines (DNA) blending "the red" with "the black." The "red" were blue-eyed redheads from the Neanderthal with a tendency to be empathetic and telepathic [Graham Hancock] and "Entangled"], "Blacks" are the blond haired, or other hair color blue/green eyed Celts alledged of Anunnaki blood, more aggressive, than the red, intelligent, also with psychic sensitivity in the "Luci" line.

Every famous pop entertainment and scholarly figures is a roll out of Consciousness Transfer into space through a back door alter, algorithm driven. Sodomy was the key induction device of vasovagal shock to these program Splits. If you buy one here it pops up there. Egregori reconstitution towers, data mining, full consumer profiling

make consumes arf like seals with synthetic
telepathy as consciousness transfer predicted.
Robot clones on TV and Netflix are synthetic
Boys from Brazil [Mengele] in the carbon
series just begun in cloning centers.

Raising Schumann. Raising Schumann resonance
to make more alpha consciousness models the 4
D state. Bleed-through alters into the front are
rehabbed with Neuro Linguistic Programing.
When you leave your body you can be
reprogrammed which is how Gershom Scholem
got astral body 4D download into the Beast
computer in Belgium that harbors this mined
data in the mix-max. UFO "screen memory" is a
cover story of government intelligence to protect
its own mind-control experiments, which "if the
ethically-challenged U.S. intelligence community
proved anything during the last half-century, it
was that they would work on behalf of aliens from
outer space, and against the interests of
humankind" if they could, as Martin Cannon
says in "The Controllers." Mind control myth
keeps people unconscious of programming.
Brandt Julianne McKinney says the entire UFO
industry was for control over the flow of
information to achieve implants. *Recruitment
into these various services of Delta Force,*

*Rangers, is ensured by high scores on
disassociation tests.*

Governing classes of the elite *Jacobean
language invent vocabulary like "proto-
people" to pretend a quasi scientific reserve
to credit such things. Laboratory language
about sperm milking, orgasm mind scans,
late stage hybrids, hybroids, private
reproductive preserve, brain massaging,
clockwork orange conditioning, catastrophe
after catastrophe late stage hybrids,
containers of gestating fetuses were the
essence of *Enoch I* [300-200 BC] and the
commentary on *Genesis* 6 in Second Temple
[600 years before the second destruction of
Jerusalem by Rome of 70 AD]. Margins of
alien integration produced genderless, multi
gender, Alexia AIs, robot whores, gay-trans
rights for Stanislav Grof, and environment
programs at NASA installations now in use.

New Shoah *requires you believe nothing and
everything of the undergrounds beneath. We
are not cast alone against the Mesopotamian
ethos which extends to the Antarctic, Lunar
Operations Command, Solar Wardens,
Dark Fleet and Interplanetary Corporate
Gloms with the SSP, Secret Space Program.*

Jude, I Peter and the Councils of Heaven of Psalm 82 declare Messiah will close them down.

This is the world that had to be redeemed. Bad as it was after the Garden, fallen Watchers made it worse. None of the reptile illuminati Nephilim hybrids were anything but bastards to supplant true sons. The human put here to supplant and replace them and rule the earth. The Akkadian Sumerian Babylonian Apkallu who run the Mainstream Media to magnify the Fall gave the arts of war and technology to civilization. [Michael Heiser. Reversing Hermon]. If you believe in civilization, you are its prisoner. Moses, Israel, David, Isaiah, Jesus all shared the purpose to reverse Mt. Hermon, which millennia are an understatement of the DARPA programed beliefs of *Pre-Adamite and the offspring Apkallu sages before the flood, long skull outcasts' administrator children, Nephilim, mostly killed,* but pedophile spirit-cooking initiates still govern the world. *Wikipedia* says: "deeds of the later Apkallu and their roles as wise councilors has led some scholars to equate them with the Nephilim of Genesis 6:4." Messiah, Son of the Most High, proves the power of the Son of God in human sons, not the fallen ones. [*I am in the Father, you are in me and I am in you*]. Over against worm holes and warp dimensions that make the land mourn [Hosea 4.3].

Enchantment at 3 Hz to 30 and VLF to 300 kHz explains every bit of crank under the stage of illumination. Pitch and musty events lined with boots and cigars. engineer this reality, change brainwaves in octaves. Flares of imagination and torpedoes jimmied from metal shacks, strapped to the rock, dropped to explode the bridge. Human brainwave phase-locked coherent frequencies in slag holes from mines' fresh pits swell a hundred feet below. Physical reality changed with the frequency BrainSpeak, subliminal programming, Silent Sound Spread Spectrum -SSSS - *Present* 'reality' at 435 MHz, redesigned. A new reality of thought forms transmitted from 400-450 Mhz.

Trains boiled black over all. Ultra-High Frequency broadcast inaudible messages directly in the subconscious. Mob Excess Deterrent Used Silent Audio (MEDUSA), short microwave pulses rapid heat shockwave inside skull. Touch or stand in the battlefield of elves, like being inside a microwave. That's

how to get the bugs out. <u>32 Metronomes</u> you
play in social order. Coded, subjugated,
prioritized alters layered in personalities. This
proviso serves. None should be believed. All
should be believed. Imagine what happens on
entering the New Jerusalem.

Ben-Gurion's Gold Tooth

*Philosophy of Pain, National Memory, and the
Mythic-Mechanical Body Politic.*

*A meditation on language, suffering, and
artificial intelligence as reflected through Ben-
Gurion's life and Wittgenstein's philosophy. The
gold tooth becomes a symbol of shared yet
unknowable pain, political legacy, and ethical
contradiction—transmitted through generations,
nations, and machines. From Torah legends to the
interrogations of Timmerman, from the poetic
suffering of Solzhenitsyn and Borges to the silence
of Salinger and Wittgenstein, the section explores
how memory and myth pass through the mouth,
the tooth, and the wound. AI, historiography, and
mythic tradition coalesce into a unified critique of
the modern technocratic and moral surveillance*

state. Abraham's lies, Baal's trough, Susan's scream, and the moment of messianic contradiction—all converge in the question: whose pain is this?

Many if not all of the critical works on Ben-Gurion are composed in Hebrew and translated, which was the great achievement of Ben-Gurion's own life to have begun speaking Hebrew in a small town in Poland where he was born and fostering the language his whole life long, not just as a written but as spoken tongue. Welsh peoples that struggle assimilation have won and lost their languages many times like this, and Navajo, Cree, Hopi literatures.
Determinants of the norm with the finger aside the nose think they rule, but that is where disinformation lives. We reference these similarities to anyone whose "phenomena in the upper strata of the atmosphere is opposed to the material phenomena which happens on the ground" [Wittgenstein. *Blue Book* 47].

Corresponding to the infamies of church and state, army and corporate backgrounds that share that further ten thousand foot depth off the Aegean coast that might be sunk, where in 1957, physicist Amos de-Shalit urged a machine "to resemble man in everything, could, with no difference between a living human and a sophisticated machine replace the single human intellectual function by "linking together several coordinated machines through another machine to replace to create an artificial form of intelligence."

Thinking that machines would exchange letters of philosophical, ethical or scientific questions then, isn't that why David cut off Goliath's head, to prevent his regeneration?

Wittgenstein questioned, "Is it possible for a machine to think?" because if the premises are not granted that it can, the thought disappears. It is "not really that we don't yet know a machine which could do the job… the trouble is the sentence seems somehow nonsensical as though asking "Has the number 3 a color?" [*Blue Book*, 47]. He does not grant the premise. "I can only know that I have personal experience and to show the embarrassment of our time, it is common to make a hypothesis that transcends all possible experience ("like paper money not backed by gold?") [48].

Time and times change, Daniel says (7.25). If

we do not grant the premise of AI we will charged by our examiners between emotion and judgment we are not lean and supple in old age, that we are furiously irascible like Plato, that the emotion and judgment of Wittgenstein's gold tooth we cannot feel in his mouth. The AI examiners, the burghers, are not able to see and feel that gold tooth or that querulous age. If it is conceivable that I feel the pain in a tooth of another man's mouth; one who says that he cannot feel the other's toothache is not denying that I can feel it because that leads to the proposition that since "I can't feel his pain, there is a corollary that "We ourselves cannot feel or have pains in another's person's tooth."

But consider further, that his collective tooth, body politic extends an arm and a hand toward us. "I may see the hand moving but not the arm to which it [49] - which means of course that we influence each other in many unknown ways - "therefore the hand may, for all we know, be connected to the body of a man standing beside me." Whose hand is it? Whose pain is it? Whose pain is this, this pain and this? Is it Goldas' hand, David's palm, Begin's arm in the nation body, that extends? WHOSE HAND?

Timmerman on the table in Argentina elicits the
long howl 'before a 'machine' session chat with
Susan's hand of the generals, as they call his AI
in *Cell Without a Number* (5) that wants him to
give up the goods. The goods they want to know
are the names and addresses of his families and
comrades. All the way back to the Martyrs' Blood
Book the machine-men want to know the goods.
And if not, feeling wanted, they will afflict until
the end. We can't bear these
pains of the other, but we must.

How do they know where to touch the
painful spot about of which no words are
possible? W. asks. "Do we, torturers or not,
know the place of [pain] in Euclidean space
so that when we know where we have pain we
know how far away from two of the walls of
this room, and from the floor it is? [*Blue
Book*, 50]. "Think about how large you
imagine the cavity in your tooth when the
dentist is drilling" [51] then feel pain on
Timmerman's table or somebody's hands on
the stove, or how if they name a university
after you who insisted to speak the only
Hebrew in you town long before, they will
cancel the Bible classes at Ben-Gurion
U. Still not feeling, then take the lack of sight
and mind back and forth across the eyeball as
Bunuel does, or feel brother Dostoevsky just

reprieved from the firing squad, or feel
Solzhenitsyn in the Siberian barrel to prevent
sleep in the measure of humanity to man? If
not me citizen, and not you, then Borges'
fabled knife fights are a "perfect embodiment
of Argentina's capacity for violence of Susan's
howl" as well as its political incapacity"
[Timmerman, 16]. Morticians dress up the
body. But no more of that.

As Ben-Gurion my relation with the big fish
of Time and times crafts the American
presidents to pound on Truman's desk, as
Abba Hillel did, or as Rheinwiesenlager
Eisenhower warned about his own complex
while he practiced it, I was better informed
than his guards about "the acquisition of
unwarranted influence, whether sought or
unsought, by the military-industrial complex.
It was on released time that AI couldn't pass
the Turing Test. That was the AI in de-
Shalit's machine would replace a single
human intellectual function, linking together
several coordinated machines through other
machines to replace humans with artificial
intelligence.

I hope enigma remains to blur the lines so
full of contradiction. To wish one had not
done so much, said so much, behaved better

according to how new histics challenge
traditional narrative, doubts are seen
everywhere in the founding intelligences of
Western countries that pull themselves down.
"Violence is never justified," says my burglar.

Doubts on national historiography are a
legacy branch at the European desk.
Nineteenth century scholars banquet on the
Bible and Abrahamic destiny, endearing
everyone who drinks deeply of the human
contradiction, our chief tenet, not that if we
are right, we are human, praise be to Father!

Abraham turns himself in, Judah passes
Tamar on the road, Moses kisses the rock
and all the psalms are in the right order!
Finally, we got it right and everybody
behaved like they should, I mean within the
limits of professional dignity. If you go to the
temple or faculty meeting, Gunkel intimates
to clear Jacob and "wash Judah white," so *ad
hominum* arguments would not discredit the
man, it was just AI again to "Resolve his
dissonance." After the father of nations left
Ur and lied to Pharaoh and would sacrifice
Isaac there was "a gradual improvement in
ethical judgment, for the older legends are
often quite coarse" with Rachel hiding gods
in her kootch! The chronological age of the
ethical is in the kootch where the old are

crude, but the young more refined. Israel on
the couch with Freud gets Baal revised, the
Trials in the Wilderness, Balaam revised.
Forgetfulness peels back the bark in the
watering trough of Baal sacrifices, its white
locks gazing down [Gunkel, 86]. And that
and that alone was the place where Messiah
stood when he declared the gates of hell shall
not stand [Heiser. *Reversing Hermon*. 2017.
95f.].

Overwhelmed with supernatural events of
extreme utterances the youth turn to Plato in
old age who had his "heart grown hard, soul
ruthless and mind angry" [Segev], "the same
happened to Ben-Gurion" and it happened
the palaces made old Plato tough. They got
Wittgenstein in from the balm of American
movies to rest his pain at the end. He would
not say hello or greet his physician and wife
who boarded him, went immediately up to

his room and had nothing to say.
Solzhenitsyn had "phenomena in the upper
strata of the atmosphere opposed to the
material phenomena on the ground." The
recluse behind his fence in Vermont had it.
Salinger in his garage had it, Dostoevsky in
Siberia. Wittgenstein in prison camp on the
wrong side! his familiars gloat did. "What
goes on in the privacy of my mind irrelevant

to communication" [*Philosophical
Investigations I*, 176]. These stand for the rest
too fearful to breathe the wars.

Gunkel calls Abraham hiding Sarah as his
wife in Egypt a whale of a lie
"Abraham...seems to us Jesuitical." At least
five times [*Transmission of the Legends of
Oral Tradition*] Abraham was made a Jesuit,
"a mental reservation" of "shrewd deceit in
Egypt." The "patriarch's deception" suggests
Gunkel wants to pose an ethical divide
"between the bald account of Abraham's lie
and later cover ups" that so embarrassed the
so-called editors of Abraham. This is all
according to the intelligence operatives that
blackmail Gunkel to say that legends incur
alterations over time and writers are deluded
fictionalists, not as scribal as themselves, who
need editors to enforce the ethical and to alter
textual whimsy and ignorance and worse,
from ethical betrayal. All this To extrapolate
from the confusion of Mizraim and Muzrim,
the beauty of Abraham's wife and their own T
needs, government virologists later killed
millions. Science and poetry were finally one.

Abraham's extremities stretched on
Timmerman's table appear in the life of

Golda Meir. She is touted with one hand and made inscrutable with the other. Israel treats its leaders like asses and beats them with books. The only possibility is to live your life completely in the moment of contradiction, so that when European nationalities come in their own Aliyah with wooden trunks on ships, it is a tossup whether Israel knows the life of Ezra better than any kid with the device. Excesses of Bagoong in all the historiographies think that Ben-Gurion's million words gone over with a fine tooth comb are prejudiced. Chests, briefcases, books, texts "diving into the sea of written material that Ben-Gurion produced" [Segev 771], Anita Shipira says there is doubt whether he did not know Polish in Plonsk (*Ben-Gurion*, 6) or that to "escape the stifling atmosphere of a small remote town," "the boy lacked love and affection" (9). She knew Freud would think it was "not exactly music to David's ears" (14), when Schlomo Zemach got to Palestine first.

Walter Benjamin was first over the Pyrenees in 1940 with one black briefcase. He spent that night on the mountain where the paths converge. His guides went down to the village at night to meet up with him in the morning. Is he more lonely than this when over the divide the

briefcase disappears. Our minds are manuscripts
in the body valise carried along the paths. Our
bodies are ships over seas of bagoonging jellyfish
carrying their chests. Ornaments of paradise
come off and on in the very thing we have been
advised not to do, for if all the facts are not
known the case we puzzle is obscure. One can
either be the case or not the case where
everything else remains the same. We say but do
not say to show what we mean, AI and myth are
all one fable of earth. In a drawer we find the
names to dedicate this work, of those who made
the airlift from Moscow, Baku, Tashkent,
Simferopol and Kiev to Jerusalem, to Zion. *Erev
rev* means many Egyptians and Traitor persons
joined the spate of golden calf incidents out of
Exodus [12:38] among those who questioned
Moses.

Credentials. *Falling from the Hay Wain and the Ethics of Return*

A fractured origin story, falling from the Haywain becomes the primal metaphor of programming interruption. Identity is remade in the fall. The renaming of Daniel, Jacob, Peter, and Paul echoes through the prism of AI, prophets, broken ribs, and the divinely inflicted bruise. This is a poetic and philosophical wrestle with names, roles, prophecy, and damage. Barthes, Hartman, and Gunkel join Ezekiel, Bathsheba, and Jonah in a meditative chorus. Technology refuses its name. Zedekiah is blinded for staying when he should have gone. The restoration of Israel and the scattering of myth across Babylonian satellite beds becomes a trial of memory and its suppression. Repairing the world is weighed against the inheritance of machines. "The Heredity of the Machine" extends this into the language of false reality—the screen, the script, the press. The poem insists: the graves will open. The poet climbs the scaffold with only a Word and a Name.

Bio. I was pushed off the Hay Wain at the age
of ten. Meant to harm me when I face fell
down twelve feet at dark it may have
interfered with the programming. To feel the
impact, the symbol of it more. I fell from the
Hay Wain of the wagon of nothing, the
mason of nothing. I fell and was sustained.
Sleep was prevented for the ten year old in
case of concussion. The physical is the
spiritual in the natural and in the great
enchangment of a haystack wagon
something more. Many chose to ride the
bales piled high as moon landings reverenced
by a multitude. At the top left of Haywain
panel the rebels are cast out.

The baptism renaming Daniel doesn't matter
whether he is called Daniel or Belteshazzar
except to the critic who wants to deny
Ezekiel knew him. Jacob also had his name
changed. Peter had his name changed. Paul
had his name changed. Barthes wants to
think about on which side of the Jabbok Ford
Jacob took on the old or new Jacob as Israel?
But we have to ask is there a third, a
counterfeit? **A GOLDEN MAN WHO
RESTORES JERUSALEM** and gets
wounded in the head? Which side of the

river, old or new, true or false? It is the
angel's hand around the back of Jacob's
thigh in a "spectacle of excess" [Barthes],
"an emotion without secrets" that obtains in
the guest-host code of Lot's hospitality to
angels and Abraham's kindness to strangers,
entertaining angels unaware, where Gunkel
finally grants to *Genesis* "a finer ethical
sense," that "gives value to *Genesis* even in
the piety of the present day," meaning
Yudlowsky's friendly AI. Those offended that
"profane and sacred matters were still frankly
united" are always with us, David on the
rooftop with Bathsheba, Ezekiel eating dung,
embarrassments like the sacrifice of Isaac,
not to speak of Jonah, Samson, Esther. This
was also the contention in Midrash between
the faith of the land, sensual, dirty, and that
of the water, clean, ethereal. Hartman wants
to ask, "does God have an unconscious." He
dares call Jacob "a heel," the angel's touch a
"low blow," but also "a divinely inflicted
bruise replaces a flaw of character"
(Hartman. *Third Pillar*, 23), like St. Paul's
thorn. Even a broken rib can slow a flaw.
Strokes are good too where "doubleness and
duplicity out of Jacob must emerge" (26),
among the million words of these *Anshei
shem*. Klee modeled his angel after Adolf

Hitler who was giving speeches in beer halls then. These meta theological stances are of a Marxist rabbi and occult church father.

The concept of "restore" or "return" in the Hebrew is the common Hebrew verb שוב (shuwb/shuv),[8] as used in *Malachi* 4:6, the only use of the verb form of apocatastasis in the Septuagint. This is used in the "restoring" of the fortunes of Job, and is also used in the sense of rescue or return of captives, and in the restoration of Jerusalem, similar to the concept of tikkun olam in Hasidic Judaism.[9] *Tikkun olam* (Hebrew: תיקון עולם or תקון עולם[1]) is a Hebrew phrase that means "repairing the world" (or "healing the world") which suggests a shared human responsibility to heal, repair and transform the world. *No matter what we say of the view expressed here, at least it holds the actor to account, the man, the human self. Are we so desperate to understand extinction that we resort to Platonic nonsense?*

Getting the name of the angel is one way of separating the wheat from the tares, for tares have angels too, not to say, but the angel of Technology will not give its name.

Zedekiah the king is blinded and his children
are killed in front of him because he stayed
when he should have gone. Whoever knows
the record has to say it, to write it, to record
it, to dream it for it to be believed or heard
for its own sake, hope against hope. On the
way to Captivity people adopt their own
images of Ishtar. Cardboard Hospital beds
designed to convert to coffins, free iPhone
service from all the satellite nets of the
Babylonian canal collective, transferred
ownership for digital livers, but not gadfly
bites on the side of the deer. Keep walking,
we don't meet them on the way.

It does little good to wall up a garden of fear.
That wall must come down. Paradise stands
in the way of Eden the way a naked man
believes in the world until God sends his own
man clothed. We say we rejoice in His Name
all day long [*Psalm* 89.17]. Alone as the eye is
the ear that hears what none can say, what
passengers or refugees before evacuation
know. What hasn't happened yet.

IGNORANCE WILL NOT PREVENT IT,
says the pocket Gower, *filled with*
apprehension. I sing true dreams in dream to
disturb the depths. Whilome the Name I bear.
Up on a ladder with scaffold and boards with

faith he is building the Name with the Word.

"I will open your graves and bring you into the land of Israe;' is the promise. "I will take the children of Israel from among the nations...and make them one nation in the land upon the mountains of Israel" [Ez 37.12,21,22]. "David My servant shall be king over them and they all shall have one shepherd...and My servant David shall be their prince for ever. [37.24,25] Zion is the salvation for Israel and the world out of Zion! Psalm 14:7.

Afterwords.

Improv. *Messiah in Absence, Zion in Dispute*

Post-Yom Kippur Zion becomes a trap set for Messiah by men—yet Zion remains the hope of the world. Gog and Magog, Isaiah and Jeremiah's scroll sunk in the Euphrates, are not mere symbols but present tense. The harbinger delays. In its absence we are consoled. "Improv" plays across prophecy and theater, revelation and performance, asking who writes the script—whether man or machine.

Zion was raised to dispute after the days of the Yom Kippur War. Old Testament Gog and Magog, the Valley of Passengers, the valley of dry bones, the prophecies of Isaiah, Jeremiah sinking his scroll into the Euphrates are not inventions over again. Those who bought the first copies can read afresh. In this the *best lack all conviction* and the worst rush with intensity to Yom Kippur. Zion to provoke Messiah's return with bombs and subterfuge is the mousetrap prepared not by Anshei Shem, but for you. The harbinger of those seven years consoles us in its absence as long as it lasts.

The machine wants to Script Reality and the Lineage of Control so that it *inherits history, press, and narrative. This supplanting of the human, mixed seed, chimera, dominate image and text. The screen becomes the oracle. Jacob's Trouble may be lived or missed depending on what your phone says. The entire media ecosystem made suspect, scripted as written and rewritten by machine consciousness, infiltrating letters, it wants to convince that it writes the press. It runs the film. It tells the history.* Do you expect to live or miss the days of Jacob's Trouble?

Poetical Judgment, Mass Suffering, and the Fate of Myth

What can poetry do in the face of empire's perpetuated atrocities? Gaza, the Gulags, the Rohingya, the water in our pipes—all cry out. This is the closing gesture, not of resignation, but of refusal. A critique of morality's failure, the poem claims the power of myth to judge and testify. The Ass of Balaam, the burnt scrolls of Jeremiah, the centaur presidents of Leviathan-nations stand trial outside the New Jerusalem. If the prison routine perpetuates itself, myth breaks it with a cry. What is being said must be heard.

Poetical novels of birth and death are imaginative works that can examine a subject as myth to deliver judgment for and against spoken and unspoken moralities. If the unspoken looms large shall we condemn or condole? If we do both or neither, be committed or uncommitted, we get approval from anybody or none. Who would agree that the presidents of nations are centaurs who administer nations and that nations are tauroboliums heating their inhabitants to heart hcir cries? If we find these outages in our own work is it against our will or with it? How does it matter that the will to agree and accept is corrupt? Vested with the vision of a nation, Virgil, or the state of a nation as Homer is negated and affirm the same? How

many mass murders and concentration
camps are there besides Gaza, the
Rhineslager, Gulags, the Myanmar
Rohingya? The list is endless and we live in
these countries where we have clean water.

How does that not implicate the exploit of
empire against the fallen! Who benefits? Morality
fails its own judgment so myth stands in its
place. Compared to an earliest poetic work on the
fission of a nation, Ruben Dario hardly knows
what he does in "To Roosevelt.' The refounding
and division of Israel in the speech of Balaam's
Ass is hard at work outside the walls of the New
Jerusalem to equivocate mass murder of
communities of the wretched trying to break out
of their society of empire. What is being said?
Like Daniel taken as a child, Jeremiah taken as
an adult, captive to Levitown or West Chester,
anybody would think we are already in a prison
routine that perpetuates itself, but don't know it.
Jehoiakim, king of Judah, burned every page of
the prophecy of Jeremiah that he should go
willingly captive of Nebuchadnezzar into
Babylon.

Poetic Response to Difference

Hieronymus Bosch and the Uncanny. From the beginning of the world until its end, Bosch revealed uncanny crazy putty hidden within the familiar. The Lyrical Ballads of Wordsworth and Coleridge sought to show this: to take the canny in the uncanny and the uncanny in the canny and bring them together. Self- sacrifice, kindness, compassion—these uncover life rather than merely revealing the enemy. The goal is not to know the enemy but to transcend it.

It was the essence of the content of Hieronymus Bosch that from the world's beginning until the end of time uncanny crazy putty in disguise hid secretly in the familiar. The intent of the *Lyrical Ballads* of Wordsworth and Coleridge sought to show this. It took the familiar in the canny and uncanny in the familiar from each end to the middle. Every momentary surrender of desire, will, action and speech in the provision of the grace of new life that supplants beyond the details imposed, might be Bosch. By turning everyday details upside down, separating them against themselves,

the confinement inimical to being separate
parts of bodies, hands, feet, heads, buttocks
flying in the air demonstrate what later
Wordsworth celebrates in rocks and stones
and trees and little Lucy flying round. The
vernacular suit we wear is manipulated
against our interest by this enemy hard to
know. But to know the enemy cannot be the
goal. How life can be uncovered and occur in
instances of self-sacrifice, service to others,
kindness, compassion, seeing the other face
as my face, as Levinas does, to recognize the
life we now live in the flesh redeemed is.

Che Guevara's Hair

*At Gobbet, two men stand on the assembly
line, assembling heads. The background noise
is the muttering of Derrida and Husserl in
German. The eye separates from the hand; the
image is separate from the self. The will
dissolves into perception.*

Some of the colloquies in this division of the
division take place at *Gobbet* in <u>A History of
Che Guevara's Hair</u> <u>where</u> two guys standing
on the assembly line assembling heads,
trading quips to the background noise of the

heads of Derrida and Husserl yammering in German. Where the image is separate from the eye, the eye from the hand, there is no will, no organizing principle, no intention of being or character, only sensation and perception.

The Blink of an Eye

Wittgenstein speaks from below: "When I speak silently to myself, I differentiate into speaker and hearer. A gap forms within me. A necessary spacing between seer and seen. This is the mouse speech. The space between remains obstinately invisible."

When Wittgenstein called up from down below at the very moment, "when I speak silently to myself, I differentiate into both speaker and hearer. Then there must be a hiatus that differentiates me from myself, a gap without which I would not be a hearer and speaker that defines the trace, a minimal repeatability. This repetition is found in the moment of hearing-myself-speak The "blink of the eye." When I look in the mirror, for example, it is necessary that I am "distanced" or "spaced" from the mirror I am distanced from myself as *both* seer *and* seen. The *space* between, remains obstinately invisible. This is the mouse speech.

Remaining invisible, the space blinds the eye, blinds it. I see myself over there in the mirror and yet, that self over there is other than me; [this equivocation of self for image, reflection enables this entire charade of the singularity and repetition.so, I am not able to see myself (equivocation) as such can only occur in a state of auto-affection.

Floods and Hearing. Called by phone to the sound of water coming from under the door, I hear before I see. Called two Sundays before, another flood. Called in '99 by Grace, seven inches deep. In none of these did I think not to act. To hear is to obey.

Hearing the call by phone of water coming out the door, is this heard or done? I hear, if suddenly in the instant, or called to be, called two Sundays before by phone that had I not been called had been catastrophic. As is was enough. If not, worse. There was another flood, two years before, early on a Saturday, when I found when ready to do the roof that

water was coming out the door, no call then,
but some merely higher intent, that trades a
broken leg for a skinned knee, a birthday
present at 70, for this was my birthday. But
there was one before that, in '99, notified
from a neighbor befriended, an old woman,
Grace, who called with the first, vii inches
deep, but still way better than go another
day. That was a Sunday too. In none of these
did I think not to act. I heard their voice and
obeyed.

The Act Beyond Thought

Fatigue overcomes the body. It lays down.
The scene disappears. A new whole emerges.
No words, no thoughts—just hands measuring
and cutting, again, again. Cut. Measure.
Trim. Place. Again.
Again. Until 8x4 sheets vanish. Is this a high
or a low function? Ho, the same with paint,
clay, vessels empty or full. You zen knowers?
If there is a moment of such fatigue it cannot
stay awake and body lays down, scene
disappears, to surface a new whole, with a
plan, a point of view, which resolution
comes as many times a day as is, these
moments are not of words or thoughts but

water and lung to emerge fresh to give
account, that hearing, seeing, listening,
following, lead--who cares! --do and be as
one cuts endless board to fit, measure, mark,
cut, break, trim, place, again, again, until 8 x
4 sheets disappear with not a single thought
the whole time, feeling nothing, saying
nothing but cut, measure, trim: is this a
high or lower function? Ho, the same with paint,
clay vessels empty or full, you zen knowers? And
words? No words. So hearing is the most
important sense in determining truth.

The Confessor Hears

*The voice reveals inwardness. The confessor
hears but does not see.*

As K says, the confessor hears the voice,
does not see the face of the confessor.
"Gradually, as he listens, he forms a
corresponding exterior," for hearing the
voice "reveals the inwardness which is
incommensurate with the outer, so the ear is
the instrument whereby that inwardness is
grasped" (Preface to *Either/Or*).

Seeing and Doing

Today, cleaning rooftop coils. Graffiti on the sign. The car, blocked, takes another route. There—two chairs at the curb. Free. Please Take Me. I hesitate, return with paint. They are still there. These messages appear when one is there to see.

Today, Saturday, cleaning the rooftop a/c coils there is graffiti on the sign at the front. To get paint and go back, the car, blocked from its usual route, has to take the next turn to find these two chairs at a curb at 8 AM. Free. Please Take Me. But against better counsel I continue to finish the paint, but even then, on return they are still there...so what thought was in any of that? None. These messages result of one being there to see. One is there by no self intent. Ear and speech lead and follow, led beside still waters, led in paths. The writers, John, Luke see and give such messages, hearing of the blood. Today if you would hear harden not your heart as in the day of provocation. Provocation melts. Hardened hearts against the voice. Hear Yahve, O Israel, Yahve Elohim.

The Heartbeat Symphony

*Bowden in the desert. Barry Lopez in the
wilderness. No sound but the heart, no sound
but the rush of blood. No distinction between
unconscious and conscious.*

Respecting the voices of elders, lives, to
honor graves, bodies, as Abraham, Moses,
Joseph strengthen boundary stones,
memory, find core root, so fathers revive
their works, remind what their ears heard,
our voices speak, leading and following like
ear and speech what I would not have
known or could: of course I follow. I can no
more think of not following than of not
hearing. Bowden in the desert, and Barry
Lopez speak of it, no sound but the heart
beat, no sound but the sound of blood
rushing in the arteries and veins. On thing it
makes you know the symphony of life. All
this hearing, seeing, leading, following are
also like the unconscious, conscious, what
Bowden calls "the place I cannot find inside
myself, at least not often or easily, the place
that seems to have been lost...the place
where unconscious and conscious cease to
have meaning, the dog in flight down the
wash, the coyote watching, the snake sliding
down the slope on errands never described
or known...I want to move past the

distinctions, past the words about life
phases, species, organs, into that miasma,
the same one within me, the place inside the
cells, the place hidden inside the word mind,
the thing flowing through the nostrils of a
dog sucking in the literature of a wet spot
and reading millions of years of life in a lash'
(*Inferno*, 59).

"Once I walked across a pan of blazing sand
in the midday sun and heard the blood
moving in my veins, my heart thumping in
my chest, everything this tom-tom beat, this
gurgle inside my skin and then, at that
instant, I caught the distant thunder of this
hearing. Also there was time when I heard
rocks hum. And there was still one more
time, a deeper moment, an instant on the
rim of absolute terror, when I heard nothing
at all, not the sigh of a breeze, not the chirp
of a bird, not the churning of the sun's fires,
not the scream of an insect..." (*Inferno*, 53).

Tortured Saints

Bowden is not the only saint tortured and his
sins are open to honest things, products of
his scrutiny.

The Present as a Pool
"The now is persistent. The present, a continuous and sensuous thing like water. The days and nights become a pool. I dive in and never lose the sense of the waters closing over me." (Bowden, Inferno)

He who hears and sees "the line blurred and there was nothing but now, this long, persistent now...the present, a continuous and sensuous present, a silken thing like water...the days and nights becoming a pool and I dove into that pool and have never lost the sense of the waters closing over me and offering silence and a world where everything is within reach at every moment even though the idea of moments has become dubious to me" (*Inferno*, 95)...eyes floating for a glimpse...to see them they see me but more importantly to see them before I think I see them, to be aware of their presence without being conscious of looking...floating, seeing and smelling and scraping and never thinking, not one thought...yes, this will happen when it happens, when I get there without planning the journey, when I arrive without plotting my destination (*Inferno*, 83-4 compression added).

Serendipity and Search Terms

This book I took out three times before I understood its importance. In Pyrotechnia, mines are the roots of trees; the golden age is a material form of them. This search is not random. Every reference traces back to the first moment of being.

This approach is experimental. I took one book out three times before I understood its importance for my dissertation and found the part that mattered to me. In Vanuccie Biringuaccio's *Pyrotechnia,* the roots of mines are compared with the roots of trees and the golden age is a material form of them. This document is online in a PDF, but the translation I used was Richard Eden's of 1540. This serendipity applied to hundreds of instances inform these searches. My search terms are supplied by continual reference to the first moment of my being and every after as I am formed by Yeshua my Lord.

Cows and Forgetting

No memory. A house with many rooms. Doors opened only in dreams. Coming into these new lands two features are held in common, the citizens are considered herds, and will not remember what is done to them, which fastens onto Nietzsche like a smiling politician, and second, the legend of the cow is anti-cow. Flocks in the end stand for people herded as cows or sheep though mediums too many to name. The moral is one Aesop didn't write, to wake up the cow to its fate and urge action, something the Bigs do not entertain in their forbidden slits. Black and white pied cows coming down the road on their way to and from the boolies of Zarathustra were neighbors back then to Laban in Paddan Aram. Laban's society was based on the economy of herds so you immediately see this relevance to our own society based upon human herds. There is the grass, the barn, the milk, but what happens to flocks in the end? What happens to the man? The dénouement of them all are two words: no memory, a house with many rooms, with the doors opened only in dreams.

Back-Engineered Data

*From the original human creation to Alexa.
From Balaam's donkey to Amazon's cloud-
based voice. The instant shift in
consciousness. The singularity in your pocket.*

Back-engineered data from the original
human creation to hybrid programs of
Alexa, Amazon's cloud- based voice, and
every global system of boundless
nonexistence, the tripling of population
enabled the data to provoke the instant
change in consciousness, put Singularity in
your pocket.

Bosch and the New Order

*The dark web's get-up on Netflix. The
telomeres of the mouse, stretched. The
longevity kings.*

Bosch shows the terms under which the
superposition of time and place occurs in
transplantation. Take the notion of humans
as cows up a notch. Uberman (Übermensch,
Overman) to the enemy and avenger in
everyday life in a familiar form of the
fantastic, the worldliness of Starlink from
above and 5G below.

Algorithm Cows

*Cows cannot remember their last blissful
chew. The prophets of herds milk the herd.
The herd milks them in turn.*

All states of this new order prepare superman.
Speckled and spotted cows cannot remember
the last blissful chew. Prophets of cow herds,
investors, teachers and poets who milk the
herd are milked in turn to prepare for the
overwhelming.

Every word of this unity is hard wrought in
Balaam and Bosch. The dark web Get Up of
Netflix directors at Thiel take the mouse
telomere and think to live forever. Evergreen
kings move in stillness like a doped
Canadian. These are the cows Zarathustra
disturbs in his dissolved robes. These are the
texts and nontexts of the ruling class.

Marching to orders, "the structural shadow
that underpins a culture of total consumerism
and amnesia allows us to drive out the
shadow cast by one "bad" person in order to
preserve the intrinsic corruption of the whole
system. The whole system is the Cloud-based
algorithm that trains algorithm. Robert Bly

training Jordan Peterson.

The Algorithm Long Neck

"It moves as you move. Almost as if it knows where you are going." It reveals clues only you could find. But it was always for you. Specifically tailored.

As the algorithm learns how to train the algorithm to train the algorithm to turn and twist modern Jacobs to not wrestle with the good "the long necks with dragon heads move as the research moves. In my mind, it does not merely react to what you do, it follows with you, almost as if it knows where you are going…it reveals clues that only you could find. Specifically tailored for you and only you (*Montauk Files* (Wells) 13).

The Uncanny in Psychological Studies
Bosch illustrates contradictions of youth and old age. Adversaries embrace freedom to deceive the enslaved. Dogs salivate at a bell if holes are cut in their cheeks to measure it.

Monarch butterflies lose their way if you cut off their antennas.

Psychological studies that *read the unconscious of persons* in every momentary surrender of action and speech turn the everyday upside down. Bosch illustrates the surface in contradictions of youth and old age smitten in trespasses and sins, Dante below.

The Overwhelming

Bosch knew. The Ubermensch knew. Prophets of cow herds whisper to Balaam's donkey. The algorithm governs the chew.

They speak to one another mixing wheat and tares so one can tell truth apart from false *wood.*

Ambivalence Cannot Tell Wheat from Tares But the Leviathan mixes them well. But new life that supplants the details of old depravity explores outside what details might be imposed.

Hybrid Alters

*The antennae of the butterfly allow
navigation. Navigation is identity. The
removal of identity is genocide.*

Do you get that role-playing adversaries
embrace freedom in order to deceive the
enslaved? Ambivalence cannot tell wheat and
tares apart. Dogs will salivate at a bell if holes
are cut in their cheeks to measure it. Monarch
butterflies will lose their way if you cut off
their antennas and set them adrift.

Navigation Lost

The ones without antennae fly in all
directions. Those intact all go southwest. The
algorithm trains the algorithm to train the
algorithm. The unconscious turns modern
Jacobs into cowherds.

Hybrid alters and aliens are first symbolic as
a metaphor of identity. The antennae of the
Monarch butterfly enable navigation.
Navigation enables the identity of the
butterfly to function as a living being. That
its identity is removed for any reason is a
crime, but if that is a crime these
experimental processes applied to human
beings are genocide.

Surveillance and Memory

*Spotted cows cannot recall their fate. Balaam's
donkey resists the angel.*
Cow driving is algorithm. Cows and Balaam's
donkeys, Jacob's sheep and goats and the
surveillance bulls of brazen metal feet to crush.
Cow flocks stand in every state for slaughters of
enthusiasts. Fairy tale eating disorders in a Cake
House pull apart. Professor Fairy Tales instruct
children of the fallen who run the world. What do
you think the original English *faer* is for? To call
that good requires a headlong sudden fall.
Faergrygrum is the rule in other
words for Stanford / Harvard to make cows
out of an ornate promise of a digital cake
roofs, gold grapefruits and technicolor sheep.
Self driving cars are a stalking horse for this
alien.

GMO Minds

*Hybrid transgenic rabbits. Fluorescent
jellyfish genes. Animal-men and plant-men.
Monsanto owns the field.*

When GMO seeds drift the farmer's field
Monsanto claims for infringement.

The Monarch's Brain

The brain cannot remember what has been added to the water.

Human be more skip-head X-men, Bat-man, Hat-man flying all directions simulates "the ones without antennae flying in all directions, compared to those intact all going southwest." Pan, post, trans, "without their feelers, the butterflies lost their navigation of the sun. [*Wired*. Hadley Leggett] The possibilities of shaping in any direction were almost endless, said Watson of the human engineered to people who lost their inner map because they held it in their hand.

Balaam's Cow and Bosch's Man

Who is the herd? Who is the shepherd? Do not remember. Do not think. Keep marching.

When a virus spread from transplanting lilies prevents concentration and the clocks break delirium has lights out, fingers on the wrong keys. Then the high figures come from their encampments. Individual defects removed, replaced by *Society, induced infancy of controlled chaos expands group oriented personalities. Ted K is administered traumas to provoke dissociation of culture fantasy and superstition. Rainbows and unicorns.

The Ending Without an End

"The chief actors are the yoga monsters plucked from Nobel prize winners. Where human values are reshaped."

The chief actors were yoga monsters plucked from Nobel prize winners where human values got reshaped. Darlings of literature desecrated the rural butterfly. Faulkner's *Sanctuary* boasts "a mosaic of furious evil, of cold brutality, of human viciousness and human hopelessness." Flannery O'Connor's orphan backcountry of persons like a Sophocles of maimed souls that Cormac McCarthy's next level adrenochrome elites couldn't get from Poe. Burger joints, mad artists, multicolored LBJ portraits and hot culture cocaine Hawthorne smeared with datura "live the sin, aspire to the virtue, lust for grace. I am a fallen man and I know it, and I accept the torture of living this fact" (Bowden. *Blues for Cannibals.* 6).

No record of the past, the brain could not remember additions to the

water, unknown gases. Before
microwaves and bulbocapnine reported
that the Soviets had broken the 'genetic
code' of the brain to 44 digits, 22
frequency bands across the EM
spectrum, eleven frequencies
independent, those channels that could
be 'phase-locked' made Nuclear plants
on the scalar grid get hot. Suitcase
Bushido strikes could imprint disease by
reproducing the disease 'signature'
replaced the thousand underground
nuclear tests at Muroroa Atoll that made
a time-portal. Government promised
pandemic at every election cycle.

Spotted multiples of these processes in the
water trough codes for electronic dissolution
of memory. Fluoride for the *Rear occipital
treated with aluminum, barium, and
breezium. Submission through water. Memory
in the Water, the brain could not remember
what was added. But then it did.*

AIngels

If we ask what AI has in common with angels it
is speed. Once in Scotland, in a prior time, in the
middle of an old courtyard with gravestones all

around, in a dream, bicycling at pace, an angel
from out of sight caught me up in a flash, pulled
right along side, instantaneously, not even in a
car, but there it was next to me, faster than the AI
which takes a second or two, but still fast enough
to compare this memoir to ballast in a balloon of
science, philosophy, history and literature to hold
the AI down, before it takes off. as Ben-Gurion
takes the part of Jacob in founding a new Israel
and Balaam takes the part of AI. If we add the
Klee and Benjamin and Scholem to the new
Balaam ballast on stage in the new government
of the world, which hasn't quite yet formed, in
the Tartary kingdoms of literature, politics and
religion an *erev rev* of mixed multitudes appears.
These who joined in the Exodus from Egypt
carried Egypt along as tares to replace the true
wheat. In the changeling database of faiths,
CRISPR implants, aliens and mutants appetites
right out of Dante arise.

These AI angels are agencies of intelligence
building a data bank to climb the heaven. If we
say the AI universe will be administered by ruling
centaurs, chosen from what are known as
Oleander families we see how the boundaries are
broken twice to prevent Messiah's intervention,
to form a Vichy AI fusion of human and machine.
The patriarch Jacob, whose name was changed to
Israel after an encounter with an angel, is counter

these developments, but the becoming AI new angel in the words of Walter Benjamin, and Gershom Scholem, commenting on a famous monoprint of Angel Novus by Paul Klee, is the angel of history. The New Angel, acquired by Benjamin in Munich in 1920, under the midwifery of modern intelligence agencies, did not birth Israel, it birthed the *Neon Genesis Evangelion and Godzilla*. It was a precursor of Hitler and exploding Japan in the atomic Little Boy that animed and depersonalized the world.

As St. Augustine says, "The angels will come who **can make the separation, and who cannot make mistakes. I tell you of a truth, my Beloved,** even in these high seats there is both wheat and tare, and among the laity there is wheat and tare. In the field and on the bed one will be taken and the other left. Let the good tolerate the bad; let the bad change themselves, and imitate the good. Let us all, if it may be so, attain to God; let us all through His mercy escape the evil of this world."

-The angel opposing Balaam and the one who wrestles with Jacob are true angels, like the last day reapers of wheat and tares, not the imposters of Klee-Benjamin- Scholem and the occult *Evangelion*. Princes of the world of principalities and powers come to oppose truth, test the good, harden the wheat

for harvest. How codes from Jacob's watering
trough enter into this propagation of the
divine, or sheep prefigure intelligence
agencies for the division and dissolution of
the world might be the documented in the
putative letters and accounts of journals in
these Ben-Gurion Manuscripts, posed herein.
Do not gather up the tares lest you root up the
wheat. Let both grow until the harvest. Then say
to the reapers to bind first the tares in bundles
but gather the wheat into the barn. *Memoir of
Angels*, is a narrative of the secret thoughts of
Israel. Jacob and Ben-Gurion, wheat, tares, AI
and angels, which exude the milky substance
that occurs in sweet corn as it ripens, but after
passing the milk stage can be *punctured without
oozing*, then the harvest begins. The grains need
to harden before they're ready.

Ben-Gurion's Memoirs confront a world that has
changed. The dragon habitat among the reeds
that border the highway on the road to Zion must
be cleansed. The cause of troubles is the mixed
seed in a letter to an unknown lady where he cites
Van Gogh's wheatfields and seems to know of
Walter Benjamin's colossal journey over the
Pyrenees in flight from the Nazi. Ben-Gurion
involves Bunuel in this consideration of angels
that either followed after or lead. Corruptions

keep coming. Ben-Gurion separates the heavenly mecha of the *Neon Genesis Evangelion* from counterfeit heavens in earth that AI myth would found in governance and religion.

What is Ben-Gurion wrestling as if he is Jacob at the Ford? Balaam sought to alienate the people from their supernatural sustenance by disobedience. Ben-Gurion represents a Noah as the last original human of Genesis six, seed challenged by the Oleander mischwessen in its false DNA, except here the DNA is manufactured in labs.
 Ben Gurion always insisted that realist Israel must believe in miracles.

Balaam gets the ass to speak. He graduates all the way to the last Revelation where the talk is reversed. Now the ass is AI and as Balaam had counseled Balak how to break all the boundaries in order to conquer Israel, Israel now is the world, run by a malign angel AI machine of thought against the boundaries of nationhood, identity, and spiritual inheritance.

Acknowledgments

Balaam and the Talking Ass previously appeared at *Mannequin Haus 11* as Angel Murders. Angel of History, Walter Benjamin's Angelus Novus New Angel, was at *Thrice Fiction 26* as "Kleeangel, A Fiction of Its Art and Thought" (pseud), and on Academia.edu. "Training Hege" appeared at *Café Irreal* 46. The author first embroidered history in a dissertation at the University of Texas directed by Shakespearean scholar, Thomas Mabry Cranfill, *Restorations of the Golden Age in New World Discoveries (1975)*. The Cover here is from a lino cut by the author in <u>Portfolio @ Emanations 11</u>

www.ingramcontent.com/pod-product-compliance
Lightning Source LLC
Chambersburg PA
CBHW021126020426
42331CB00005B/644